THE NO-GOOD PREACHER

Serving God  Despite All Odds

Charles White With Lois Moore

REVIEW AND HERALD® PUBLISHING ASSOCIATION
Since 1861 | www.reviewandherald.com

To order additional copies of *The No-Good Preacher,*
by Charles L. White, call 1-800-765-6955.

Visit us at **www.reviewandherald.com**
for information on other Review and Herald® products.

Copyright © 2010 by Review and Herald® Publishing Association

Published by Review and Herald® Publishing Association, Hagerstown, MD 21741-1119

Review and Herald® titles may be purchased in bulk for educational, business, fund-raising, or sales promotional use. For information, e-mail SpecialMarkets@reviewandherald.com.

The Review and Herald® Publishing Association publishes biblically based materials for spiritual, physical, and mental growth and Christian discipleship.

The author assumes full responsibility for the accuracy of all facts and quotations as cited in this book.

Texts credited to NIV are from the *Holy Bible, New International Version.* Copyright © 1973, 1978, 1984, International Bible Society. Used by permission of Zondervan Bible Publishers.
Texts credited to NKJV are from the New King James Version. Copyright © 1979, 1980, 1982 by Thomas Nelson, Inc. Used by permission. All rights reserved.

This book was
Edited by Steven S. Winn
Copyedited by James Hoffer
Cover design by Ron J. Pride
Interior design by Johanna Macomber
Typeset: Bembo 11/13

PRINTED IN U.S.A.
14 13 12 11 10   5 4 3 2 1

Library of Congress Cataloging-in-Publication Data
White, Charles L., 1920-
   The no-good preacher : serving God despite all odds / Charles L. White ; with Lois Moore.
      p. cm.
   1. White, Charles L., 1920- 2. Seventh-Day Adventists—United States—Biography. I. Moore,
Lois. II. Title.
   BX6193.W45A3 2010
   286.7'32092—dc22
   [B]
                                        2009037315

ISBN 978-0-8280-2470-9

CONTENTS

"You'll never amount to a hill of beans—
nope you'll never amount to anything!"

HOW IT ALL STARTED

I felt that the week-long series of religious meetings at the church-run high school had failed! After each meeting I sat in an office waiting to provide individual support for the young people's spiritual needs, but only one or two came. On Thursday evening I could not resist the prompting of the Holy Spirit, so, abandoning my planned topic, I started sharing the story of my life. Almost immediately, young people were leaning forward in their seats, many of them unashamedly wiping tears from their eyes. God was speaking to them through my story!

I opened up the program for the young people to share how God was working in their own lives, and one student after another approached the microphone. Soon, the line of those waiting to speak ran clear down the side aisle to the back door. I glanced at my watch, and then at the principal. He signaled to let the meeting continue. We should have closed at 8:30, but at 9:00, then 9:30, and almost until 10:00 that evening, the young people testified of God's faithfulness and of their own commitment to Him.

After that meaningful experience I knew that I must tell my story to as many as possible. Though God had performed many miracles in my life, writing a book proved to be one miracle He did not perform! I wrote out my story and submitted it to several publishing houses, but all refused it. In discouragement I spoke with one person and then another. Somehow Lois Moore heard about my manuscript, read it, and offered to help put it in book form. Thus, God has enabled my story to be transferred from the murals of my experience to the pages of this book, and, I hope, to the inner recesses of your heart.

While the entire book is based on facts, some minor scenes and dialogue have been altered and some names changed to make the story flow more easily, and to protect the guilty!

The older I grow the more convinced I become that there is no one—I repeat, *no one anywhere*—who, when God becomes central in their lives, cannot achieve their dreams. God tells us, "I know the plans I have for you, . . . plans to prosper you and not to harm you, plans to give you hope and a future" (Jer. 29:11, NIV).

God has more than fulfilled His promise in my life! I pray that as you read my story, you will come to know that no matter what your past has been, no matter how unlikely it seems that you can succeed, you will realize as I finally did that "I can do all things through Christ who strengthens me" (Phil. 4:13, NKJV).

So come journey with me through the ups and downs of my life. And may you and I both stand together one day, looking up into the sky, to welcome our coming King!

—*Charles L. White*

Chapter 1

WELCOME TO THE WORLD

Emily pulled her faded yellow apron to her face and wiped the sweat from her brow. "Cooking on a wood stove just makes too much heat for September," she sighed. She straightened her back and tried to rub away the ache. A sudden twinge of pain made her catch her breath.

Seven-year-old Harold looked up as he heard Emily's gasp. His neatly patched jeans and old T-shirt hung on his thin frame like a dressed scarecrow. He shoved aside his reading book. He had noticed his mother moving slower and slower the last few weeks. *What was wrong with her?* he wondered.

Emily saw his worried look and smiled in spite of her pain. "It's OK, son. I'll be fine," she assured him. "Now get back to your reading." She pushed back a few wisps of gray hair that showed among the brunette ones. Because her hair was curly, it refused to stay in a tightly twisted bun, and ringlets framed her lined brow. She dearly loved each of her children, those still at home and her two grown daughters. Life had been good to the Whites, who had come to Colorado shortly after their marriage.

Bertha, two years younger than Harold, came screaming into the house, her two braids flying behind her. "Mama! Make Lloyd stop hitting me! He's so mean!" Bertha looked just like her mother—same brunette hair, blue eyes, angelic face, and dainty hands. Even in her brown corduroy coveralls, she was the picture of femininity. Emily frowned at Lloyd who burst through the door behind his sister.

"She won't play cowboys and Indians with me, and Ray and Lawrence are too little," he complained. Although small for his age, Lloyd had just turned 4 and felt much older than his little brothers. Ray, at 3, was not much bigger than 1 1/2-year-old Lawrence. Just yesterday, Lloyd had tried to tie up Bertha, telling her that he was an Indian brave and she was his captive. Her screams had brought Emily waddling as fast as she could to rescue her poor daughter.

Emily grimaced as another pain gripped her. She leaned forward and suppressed a groan. Harold, Lloyd, and Bertha all noticed her tense up and catch her breath. Instinctively, Emily placed her hands over her swollen belly and felt the baby kick against her ribs.

The stew gently bubbled on the back of the stove and the aroma of hot biscuits perfumed the kitchen. But supper would have to wait, because this baby wasn't going to! Having delivered 15 children, Emily knew that it wouldn't be long. *Why,* she wondered, *is Charles insisting that this baby be born in the hospital?* All her other children had been delivered at home.

"Harold. Go get Daddy quickly. Tell him that Mommy is having bad pain."

Thankful to leave his reading lesson, Harold scuttled out of the house in search of his dad.

Where is Charles? Emily wondered. *He'd better hurry, or this baby will be born right here at home anyway!*

Just then Charles came racing into the house, panting, hoe still in hand. "Charles, put the hoe down!" Emily laughed in spite of her condition.

Charles instructed Harold to walk himself and the four younger children to Aunt Lottie's house, just two blocks away. Dear aunt Lottie! A professional secretary, she prided herself on her skills. Always on time to work, she never failed to meet or exceed a deadline. Like Charles, she had jet-black hair, which she combed into a bun. She always looked the picture of perfection in her dark suit, stiffly starched blouse, and sturdy shoes. One of Charles' two younger sisters, she was always ready to help out in a pinch. His other sister, Lois, taught school and didn't have as much spare time as Lottie did.

Tossing Emily's prepacked satchel into the back seat of their old Model T with one hand, Charles helped her climb into the front seat with the other. In 1920, Model T Fords were still common and Charles and Emily felt fortunate to own one—along with the work truck. Both vehicles were black. The upholstery in the Model T had tape covering several rips, and the floorboards would have allowed water to splash in had Emily not laid down an oilcloth and covered it with a tattered piece of carpet. The truck showed even more signs of wear—the water did splash up through the floorboards, and one headlight had been wired into place over a bent-up front fender. Charles kept them both in good running condition, so he knew the trip to the hospital would be mechanically uneventful.

As Charles tried to back out of the driveway as smoothly as possible, Emily looked over at their house. *Home,* she thought. The exterior paint almost matched the faded apron she had forgotten to take off. The three oldest boys shared one tiny bedroom only because that room had a trundle that slid underneath the bunk beds. Bertha and baby Lawrence shared another bedroom with hardly enough room to move between the two cots. She and Charles' postage stamp-sized room held their double bed, which, when shoved against the wall, allowed just enough room for a cradle for each newborn.

Home. Enough food, hand-me-down clothes, and lots of love and good times. Home. A happy place, even though Charles had to work long hours to make enough money to survive. Though he worked hard, Charles made time to play with his sons and teach them as they worked at his side.

As the Model T bumped along the dirt road toward the hospital, Emily reflected over her past 20 years of marriage to her dear Charles. Their move to Colorado Springs had brought many changes, as Charles began farming their newly bought small acreage. He'd learned a good bit about farming during those years, and the crops improved each year. He had to take odd carpentry jobs in addition to the farm work to make ends meet.

They had been difficult years, as well. Emily still grieved for the eight children who had died either as infants or in early childhood. She thought fondly of their two older daughters who had survived, one of whom was now married, making her a grandma to three. Their own "younguns," as Charles fondly called them, were about the same age as their grandchildren.

Harold proved to be her right-hand helper. "True blue," she called him. Dependable and honest, he showed consistent kindness to his younger siblings. Bertha, age 5, suffered being the only girl, tormented at the hands of both Lloyd and Raymond! Baby Lawrence enjoyed Bertha's motherly care and any attention he got from his older brothers. *Quite a family,* Emily mused.

Fortunately, the hospital was only a couple of miles away, and there was virtually no traffic to impede their progress. Charles pulled up to the emergency entrance and called for someone to help. No one seemed to hear, so he helped Emily out of the car, leaving it parked at the entrance. Arm in arm, they hurried inside as fast as Emily could waddle.

The smell of rubbing alcohol and other hospital smells assaulted their nostrils as they entered the emergency room. Taking one look at Emily, one of the nurses, in her stiffly starched white uniform and nurse's cap, grabbed a wheelchair and began wheeling her to the labor and delivery room. "Go park your car and then you can come back," the nurse called to Charles over her shoulder.

Graying at the temples and portly in size, Dr. Herdt carried himself erectly. His kindly eyes belied his take-charge demeanor, and as soon as he walked in, Emily felt that she was in good hands. As soon as the labor and delivery nurse briefed him on Emily's condition, he strode to the sink to scrub his hands before donning a sterile gown and gloves.

Charles paced back and forth in the waiting room, feeling useless, yet wanting to be near just in case he was needed. He whispered, "Oh God Almighty, you have blessed us with 15 children. Let this one be healthy, especially since half of my children have died so young. Bless the only two who have seen adulthood and bless my five little ones at Lottie's place until we can all be together again."

Half an hour passed. Expectant fathers seem to share a penchant for worry, and Charles was no different. *What if . . . ? How come it's taking so long?*

"You're going to wear a hole in that floor." Dr. Herdt's approach interrupted Charles' anxious thoughts. Still wearing his green gown, now stained with blood and certainly no longer sterile, he walked up to the weak-kneed, wide-eyed husband. Charles hurriedly caught the edge of a chair as Dr. Herdt announced, "Congratulations, Charles! You have another baby boy. What are you going to name him?"

"We'd, we'd hoped for a girl," Charles stammered, "and were going to name her Charlene. We haven't picked out a boy's name. I guess we've run out of boys' names!"

"Charlene. Hmmm. Well, how about 'Charles'?" Dr. Herdt suggested. "You don't have a 'Charles, Junior' yet."

"Charles . . . Charles. Yes, I like that," Charles said, nodding his head. "I guess that'll make me Charles, Senior, won't it?"

After Emily was cleaned up she was wheeled into a room with two other mothers. All the moms in the maternity wards of those days were supposed to sleep at the same time, awaken at the same time, and feed their babies at the same time. The maternity ward smelled just as sterile as the rest of the hospital, and Emily wondered silently why it was supposed to be so much better than delivering at home. She missed Charles' two spinster sisters, Lottie and Lois, hovering around. She missed the sight of the other children gingerly touching the baby, fearing that he might break! She missed Charles being right there with her, and she missed her own bed! Still, she was thankful that Charles cared enough to provide the very best that their budget would allow.

During visiting hours that evening, Charles asked, "What do you think, Emily? Dr. Herdt suggested that we name the baby Charles, and I kinda like it."

"Charles . . ." Emily murmured thoughtfully. "Yes! I like it, too." Thus, Charles White, Junior was named. "Let's call him 'Little Charlie,'" Emily suggested, "so we won't get confused about which Charles we mean."

Just then, the nurse brought Little Charlie in to his parents. He was wrapped tightly in two white receiving blankets, with just his head visible. Emily eagerly unwrapped Little Charlie and began inspecting him. She counted his fingers and toes and felt the soft spot on his head. He had only a little hair, but it was black, just like his dad's. Just when she decided that he was normal, he coughed. It was a weak, whiney cough, which made her notice that his breathing and cry weren't very strong, either. Visiting hours over, Charles left for home, and Little Charlie was whisked back into the nursery.

Emily fell into a troubled sleep. She just didn't like the sound of Little Charlie's breathing, his cough, or his cry. She decided she would ask Dr. Herdt about him in the morning.

Dr. Herdt agreed that Little Charlie's lungs were not as strong as those of other newborns, but he hoped that after a few days of good breast milk and rest from the delivery process, he would improve.

Normally, women were kept in the hospital for up to a week, but Charles convinced Dr. Herdt that he would be able to care for Emily at home. Dr. Herdt reluctantly discharged both Emily and Little Charlie on the fourth day, admonishing Charles to keep the baby warm and away from drafts of air, and to keep Emily in bed.

Little Charlie didn't improve much. During his checkup three days later, Dr. Herdt softly informed his parents, "I'm afraid he's going to be a sickly baby."

"Well, Lord," Charles prayed aloud after the door closed behind Dr. Herdt, "we prayed for a healthy baby. We don't understand why Little Charlie has to be sickly, but we pray for wisdom to know how to raise him. Thank You that Emily is regaining her strength. And thank You for the bumper crop of potatoes that will soon be ready to harvest."

With six children to support, Charles was thankful for his carpentry skills that were needed now more than ever to augment the income from their small Colorado farm. Emily helped when and where she could, but she had her hands pretty well full with her family of now five boys and one girl.

As she sat in their rocking chair nursing little Charlie and humming softly to him, Emily heard Charles come up the back stairs. She thought his steps sounded a little slower than usual, and she missed his cheerful whistle. As he entered the room, he stooped and planted a kiss on her forehead. Reaching out to give his worn, calloused hand a tender squeeze, she noticed that his broad shoulders, usually erect, were now stooped. Worry lines had dug themselves into his forehead, and the light in his eyes had dimmed.

"What's wrong, Charles?" she asked.

"Well," he sighed, "Um . . . oh, everything will be OK." It was obvious that he wasn't telling her what was really on his mind, but she decided not to push him.

The next morning, as she sat in the squeaky rocking chair nursing nine-day-old Little Charlie, her mind drifted. *Why had Charles evaded her question? Why had he looked so worried?* She was crooning a soft lullaby when she suddenly lost all her strength, gasped for air, and slumped in her chair. The monotonous squeak of the rocking chair ceased as Little Charlie slid from her arms to her lap.

Bertha had been standing beside the rocker, stroking Little Charlie's head. "Mommy! Mommy!" she screamed, but Mommy's only reply was to drop her head to one side and slump deeper into the chair. Bertha grabbed Little Charlie, put him on the floor, then tore out of the house, yelling, "Daddy! Come quick! Daddy!"

Chapter 2

TRIPLE TRAGEDY

By the time Charles came racing into the house, Emily's lips were blue. He reached for her hand. It lay mottled and limp in his palm. Bending to put his ear to her chest, he heard nothing, and she wasn't breathing. Frantic, he jumped in the Model T and raced to the hospital, where he hoped Dr. Herdt would still be making his rounds.

"Dr. Herdt! Dr. Herdt! Come quickly!" he cried as he rushed into the emergency room. "Dr. Herdt, there's something terribly wrong with Emily." The doctor followed Charles to their home in his own car.

By the time they reached the house, Harold had picked Little Charlie up from the floor and was trying to rock him to stop his weak cry. Dr. Herdt checked Emily's pulse, listened to her chest, gently spread her eyelids and peered into her now dilated pupils, then pressed his stethoscope again to her chest. He shook his head slowly. "Charles, she's gone. She's dead. I suspect a blood clot, or 'milk legs,' as they call it. The clot must have immediately shut down her lungs, though I can't know for certain."

Charles stood dumbfounded and couldn't move. His eyes seemed to be staring at some far-off land, and he was unaware of the questions tumbling from his children's quivering lips.

"Daddy, what's wrong?" Harold asked.

Daddy didn't answer.

"Daddy, what happened?" Bertha persisted. "Mommy was rocking Little Charlie and then she just dropped him in her lap." She took sleeping Little Charlie from Harold and gently laid him in his cradle.

Dr. Herdt realized that Charles was in shock. "Harold, take your brothers and sister to your Aunt Lottie's," he commanded rather sternly. "She should still be home. I don't think she leaves for work till about 8:30. All you kids, go. *Now.*"

Harold, the suddenly grown-up little man, picked up Lawrence. "Bertha, hold Lloyd and Ray's hands, and all of you follow me," Harold commanded. They marched solemnly out of the house, leaving Little Charlie sleeping in his crib where Bertha had laid him. Harold commented, "Dad, we're going to Aunt Lottie's like Dr. Herdt told us to. Please come get us real soon." Then he and his siblings headed out the door.

Charles still stood like a statue, not moving, barely breathing. He slumped into the nearest chair and finally managed to stammer, "Wha . . . what is happening?"

"Charles, Emily is dead," Dr. Herdt repeated, hoping that a repetition of the fact would bring him back to reality.

Charles' eyes shifted from his far-off land to the doctor. "No! It can't be," he groaned. He stood, walking on shaky legs over to his pale wife. "No! Emily . . . *Emily*, can you hear me?" he shouted into her ear while shaking her shoulder.

"Charles, it won't do any good. I am so terribly sorry. She's gone. She died before I got here." Dr. Herdt gently removed Charles' hand from Emily's shoulder and led him to a chair by the table. "Charles, the only thing we can do now is plan for your future without Emily."

Charles laid his head in his hands and wept aloud. "It can't be! No! I can't believe it," he gasped between sobs. Yet even as he said the words, he had to believe that it really was true—his Emily was dead.

"What in the world do you mean, sending Harold and the other kids over to my house?" Lottie shouted as she stormed into the house. Her face was a thundercloud discharging its bolts. But when she saw Dr. Herdt and Emily's prostrate form, she stopped in her tracks. "Oh, Charles! Harold only told me that Emily was sick! What happened?"

Dr. Herdt quietly answered, "We don't know exactly what happened, but Emily has died very suddenly. I didn't know what else to do with the children, so I sent them to you. I didn't want them to see their mother carried out to a hearse. I will need to call the mortuary to come pick her up. Is there some way you could keep the children until they have come and removed Emily?"

Lottie, like Charles, was dumbfounded. Neither could find words. Finally, she gave the slightest nod and managed to squeak, "Of course." She sat down beside Charles and they wept together. Little Charlie's weak cry and pitiful coughing soon joined their somber duet. Lottie picked him up and sniffed, "I'll take him, and I'll send Bertha or Harold to buy some baby bottles and formula." Her voice trailing off, she cradled him in her arms and left.

"I was hoping Lottie would help prepare Emily before the mortician arrived," Dr. Herdt said, but I guess you will have to, Charles. I know this will be terribly hard for you. Here, I'll help ease her to the floor. Then you need to wash her up, roll a towel to put under her chin, and fold her hands across her chest." After Emily was on the floor, Dr. Herdt closed her eyes, apologized that he could not stay, and left to call the hearse.

Later that day, Charles, still in a daze, went to town to arrange for the sale of his potatoes. Alas! His worst fears were realized. Everyone, it seemed, had planted potatoes. All, like he, had had bumper crops and potatoes flooded the market. It would cost more to harvest them than he could gain from their sale!

"Oh my God, why have You forsaken me?" Charles wailed as he drove home. "First, we prayed for a healthy baby, but Little Charlie is sickly with weak lungs. Then, You take my dear Emily. And now, I won't make any profit at all from my potato crop! Where are You, God? What is going to happen to my family?"

Gripping the steering wheel, he thought, *Well, at least the kids and I won't starve. We can eat potatoes and potatoes and more potatoes.* He chuckled in spite of his triple tragedy. "Thank You that we can have potato soup, potato salad, mashed potatoes, and maybe even potato porridge for breakfast. Somehow, I know You are going to see us through this black veil of tears."

Chapter 3

THE FUNERAL

The day of the funeral dawned warm and clear. The sun shone from a nearly cloudless sky. What a perfect day for anything but a funeral! It could have been a happy reunion, since both of Charles' older daughters, Elizabeth with her husband Andrew, and Clara with her fiancé Thad, had come. Normally, Charles loved to romp and play with Elizabeth's three children, but today he didn't even seem to notice them. Today's occasion certainly held no joy!

The funeral service in the church seemed surreal to Charles. The music, the eulogy, the sermon . . . they were like a horrible nightmare from which he longed to awaken. Together with his two daughters and all the children, they made their way from the church to the graveyard for the interment.

Daddy Charles held Little Charlie close to his shabby black suit and patched white shirt, sobbing audibly, his shoulders shaking with each gasping breath. Harold held Ray's little hand, and whispered, "It'll be OK, Ray, it'll be OK," even as he sucked in air between his own sobs. Bertha, her hair tangled from two days of poor attempts at brushing, hid behind Charles' pant leg while Lloyd crouched beside the open hole in the ground and Lawrence wandered forlornly, bewilderment on his face.

"What is going on? Why is everyone so sad?" Lloyd wondered out loud. "Where's Mommy?" he asked into the air. His adult sisters, having their own children to tend to and struggling with their own questions, didn't know how to answer him, so he just stood sadly beside Harold.

Charles nearly collapsed as the coffin was lowered into the ground. His two sons-in-law, Andrew and Thad, supported him. Andrew lifted Little Charlie from his arms and handed him to Elizabeth.

"Dust to dust, ashes to ashes," intoned the minister, and then someone threw a few rose petals on top of the coffin. Charles tore himself and his bereft family away from the grave before the clods of dirt started pelting the casket of his beloved Emily. After the funeral, the family gathered at Aunt Lois' house for lunch. No laughter. No light banter. Most could hardly even eat.

"What are you going to do about baby Charles?" his older daughter Elizabeth asked. Lois and Lottie both chimed in, "Yes, what will you do? It'll take a lot of time to care for the little one."

"Oh, I can manage. I'll take care of him," Charles replied.

Elizabeth and her husband Andrew looked knowingly at each other, both realizing that Charles had not a clue how many hours a newborn baby required! In addition to nighttime, morning, afternoon, and evening feedings, there would be bottles and diapers to wash, plus the care of five little children all under the age of 7! The family recognized that all this, added to running the farm and doing odd carpentry jobs, did not paint a realistic picture. They tried to reason with him, but he was too deep in shock to be able to think clearly.

Aunt Lottie stepped over and laid her hand on Charles' shoulder. "Charles, would it help if I took Little Charlie home with me? Elizabeth and Andrew have children of their own to tend, and Clara is planning her wedding, and . . ."

"No, no. He's the last part of Emily that I have left. No. Somehow I'll—we—we'll manage, Charles said matter-of-factly. Realizing further discussion was useless at the moment, one by one the family bade Charles and the younger children goodbye.

That evening, Charles surveyed his little brood. "Harold, you are the oldest one here. You'll have to be my helper boy. No more cowboy and Indian games with Bertha," he added as he tousled Harold's hair.

"Yes Dad," Harold replied soberly.

"And Bertha, even though you are just 5 years old, you can be a mama for baby Charlie." Bertha's eyes grew round with both fear and pride. "I'll take good care of the baby," she vowed.

How bravely Charles and the children tried to manage! The church folks kindly brought casseroles, vegetables, and bread enough to last for about a week. As that food began to run out, Charles, who knew almost nothing about cooking, prepared the two things he knew how to fix: oatmeal mush for breakfast and boiled potatoes for lunch and supper. Two weeks later, all the children were sick and tired of the fare. Although they were good kids and had been taught to not complain, Harold whispered to Bertha, "I sure wish Dad knew how to fix something else!" Lloyd and Lawrence, not so diplomatic, chorused, "Not that again!" And Raymond? He just pouted and said, "No good."

Bottles to be sterilized, formula to be made (Charles had never even seen formula prepared before—all their babies had been nursed), diapers to wash, and the care of his five older children, required more time than he could find in a 24-hour day! Arguments between the kids, dirty clothes piling up, unwashed dishes in the sink (that had running water only if you ran with a bucket of water from the well), and the catch bucket under the drain to be carried out before it overflowed . . . it was all just too much! Harold tried to help, but what could a 7-year-old boy do? Bertha rocked Little Charlie and learned how to change his diaper, but no one could fill the shoes of their beloved mother and wife.

And the farm. Even though he couldn't afford to harvest the potatoes, he knew that they needed to be dug. The late season tomatoes, string beans, peppers, cucumbers, and squash all demanded attention, too. "How did Emily ever find time to do the canning?" Charles wondered. His energy sagging, he knew something had to change.

Charles raised his weary hand and knocked on Lottie's front door.

"Lottie, you offered to take Little Charlie but I wonder if you could come to my house and help me out. It's impossible for me to care for him by myself, and keep the family all together." Leaning against the door frame, the exhaustion and worry overtook him and the tears flowed. "I was just wondering . . . could you maybe come and help out for a while?"

Lottie smiled. "Charles, maybe it would be better if I just took Little Charlie," she said. "If you could get a babysitter to care for him while I'm at work . . ."

Back home, the five older children stared wide-eyed as Daddy gathered up Little Charlie's diapers, bottles, hand-me-down blankets, and baby clothes and put them in a cardboard box. A chorus of crying began as Aunt Lottie left with their baby brother in her arms.

Chapter 4

OUT OF CONTROL

When was the last time I've slept through an entire night? How could one little baby take so much time? Lottie's thoughts tumbled in her weary mind. Charles had found a babysitter for Little Charlie while she was at work, but the teenage girl always wanted to leave the minute Lottie walked in the front door, and taking care of the little guy just in the evening and nighttime was wearing her out. Sometimes she fell asleep while giving Little Charlie his bottle.

Worn out after a month, she decided to take Little Charlie to Lois for a while.

"Lois," Lottie blurted out as soon as her sister's front door opened. "I've got Little Charlie here, and he's a precious baby, but . . ." Younger than Lottie, and a schoolteacher, Lois loved children. Even though she was only five feet tall and "barely a hundred pounds soaking wet," as Charles teased, she expected and received the respect of her pupils, who also loved her for her gentle side.

Lottie continued. "As you know, Charles asked me to take care of Little Charlie for a while, because he can't handle it. He thought that because I wasn't married, I could help him out. But I'm exhausted from so little sleep. Could you maybe take Little Charlie for a while? I'll bring over his diapers, formula, and clothes. Here. Please take him," she said as she placed him in her arms. "After all, you aren't married, either."

"Lottie, I just happen to teach school, remember?" Lois remonstrated as she accepted the little tyke into her arms. "Don't think that I have more time than you do. You leave the office at five and your work is done. I bring work home nearly every day," she sputtered.

"I know. But I just can't keep this up. I'm near collapse."

"You don't think you're exaggerating just a bit?" chuckled Lois.

"I'm not exaggerating! I'm more than half dead! Please Lois. Just for a few days."

With a sigh, Lois looked down at Little Charlie's peaceful little face, then back at her sister's desperate expression. "OK," she mumbled. "I'll help out—but just for a few days, mind you."

When Lois returned from school the next afternoon, there were lesson plans to prepare, papers to grade, new bulletin boards to create, concerns about the slow student—a seemingly endless list. But now she was faced with another list. She needed to make food for Little Charlie (there were no premade baby foods back then), feed him, talk to him, and play with him, on top of her own household chores. How could she care for him and not fall behind in her work? Like Lottie, she soon felt drained, too. The sisters tried sharing the load; one kept Little Charlie while the other did the shopping and laundry. As that plan fell apart, Lois had to admit that Lottie had not been exaggerating at all.

Ping-ponging from Lottie to Lois and back continued for more than a year and a half.

One evening, Lois sat down at her small, wooden table to prepare the next day's lesson plan when Little Charlie tottered by dragging his box of toys. "Play," he said, staring at her expectantly.

"No, Charlie. You have to go to bed now," she commanded. "It's time to take your bath and then go to sleep."

"Play with ducky in bath?" he tried.

"No! Auntie said No! Stop being such a bad boy!" she said sharply.

"Not bad boy. Me good boy. Want to play," he wailed.

She didn't play "this little piggy went to market" with his toes. She didn't read him stories. When she tried to hurry him, he only cried harder. Many times, as he sat screaming at the top of his lungs, she would give him a piece of candy, a cookie, or whatever he wanted, just to quiet him down. She knew in her heart of hearts that she wasn't doing a very good job of being his mommy.

For another year, Little Charlie moved from here to there. He'd spend a while with Aunt Lois, then be carted off to Aunt Lottie's. Sometimes he'd spend a little while back with his dad and siblings, but he had no permanent home.

As Charlie grew physically, both Lottie and Lois knew that he wasn't getting the emotional nurturing he needed. One afternoon, Lottie arrived at Lois' house just as Lois returned from school, arms loaded with papers, books, and projects.

"Lois, we have to do something about this," Lottie said. "It isn't fair to Little Charlie to be shifted from one place to another. He has no mommy, and he doesn't know where he belongs. He's becoming a spoiled little brat that none of us know how to manage other than give in to him. He needs consistency. He needs discipline."

"I've been thinking the same thing," Lois confessed as she pushed open the door and plopped her things on a chair.

"I was wondering what you'd think of running an ad in the *Central Union Reaper*. People all over Colorado and several other states would see it, and it may be just what we need."

Lois furrowed her eyebrows and looked at her sister. "What kind of an ad? You mean for a nanny?"

Lottie paused, then said solemnly, "No, I was thinking of putting him up for adoption."

"Adoption!" Lois gasped. "We can't do that! He doesn't even belong to us. Only Charles could do that."

"I know, but what can we do?" Lottie's hands flew up in exasperation.

As they talked, they knew that Charles would never consent to putting Little Charlie up for adoption, yet they saw no other good alternative. After a long discussion, they decided to submit the ad and not discuss anything with Charles until someone appeared ready to adopt Little Charlie. The next week, their terse ad appeared in the church newspaper: "Little boy for adoption. 2 1/2. Contact Lottie White for more information . . . Colorado Springs, Colorado."

"I don't know what we'll say to Charles if someone responds," Lois worried.

"Well, we'll cross that bridge when we get to it," Lottie said matter-of-factly.

Neither of them realized it at the moment, but the bridge would come sooner than they expected. Someone in a distant city saw their ad.

Chapter 5

STILL AVAILABLE

In Lincoln, Nebraska, Anna sat listlessly rocking in her squeaky wooden rocker by the fireplace. Winter's icy grip held Lincoln, and most of Nebraska, hostage to the cold, and it seemed that spring would never come. Anna, still grieving the loss of her only son several months ago, sat day after day, waiting for "spring" to come back into her life. Just the day before, her doctor had told her, "Anna, you can never bear another child." That crushing blow threatened to settle winter forever in her heart.

Anna had completed a college degree in education and had taught school for several years before she and Lewis married. Soon after leaving her teaching career to devote herself to motherhood, the death of her precious newborn began a steep decline in her life. She began to put on weight by nibbling incessantly on truffles and bonbons. Bowed down with sorrow, the thought of cooking nourishing meals for herself and her husband overwhelmed her, and she often didn't even get dressed until late afternoon. Many days she didn't brush and arrange her long brown hair. Her glowing, rosy cheeks faded to match her gray eyes, which often spilled tears down her pretty face. Because Lewis was blind, Anna convinced herself that it didn't matter how she looked.

The furniture throughout the house wore a thick mantle of dust, the linoleum on the kitchen floor needed mopping, the rugs hadn't been shaken and beaten for weeks. The dishes Lewis had used the last several days remained unwashed in the kitchen sink.

"My baby, my precious baby—gone!" Anna would sob. "I'll never be able to hold him again. It's not fair! It's just not fair! Whisked away by pneumonia when he was so little! And now the doctor tells me I can't ever get pregnant again. It's more than I can bear!"

Lewis loomed large at six feet three inches and 300 pounds. Although completely blind, every day he walked with his white cane the several blocks from their house to the print shop where he worked repairing printing presses for the Christian Record Blind Association. He could tell just by listening whether the machines were running smoothly or not, and he could take a machine apart, service and clean it, and put it back together faster than many sighted men. His large, strong, and somewhat portly frame strained his shirt buttons. That, combined with his remarkable success at overcoming obstacles gave him a powerful presence, and yet he felt absolutely powerless to help his wife out of her depression.

One evening, Anna sat in her rocker reading a church newspaper as flames slowly devoured a knotted piece of wood in the fireplace. Jerking her head, she rattled the paper and squinted her eyes to be sure she was seeing the ad right. "Lewis! Lewis, look at this! Come quick!"

In the other room, Lewis frowned at the interruption to his favorite radio program. "What?" he grunted, still focused on the radio.

"Look! Little boy for adoption," she read aloud, ". . . 2 1/2. Contact Lottie White for more information . . . Colorado Springs, Colorado. Oh, Lewis, do you suppose . . . do you think . . . I mean, might this be the way to have a family?"

Lewis sighed, switched off the radio, and felt his way into the living room, and she read the ad to him again. Then she asked, "What do you think?"

After a thoughtful moment Lewis replied, "Look Anna, we have no idea what kind of habits this boy may already have developed. We don't know his heredity. We don't know if he's mentally retarded or crippled or if he has some terrible disease. We just don't know anything about him."

"Well, we could write and find out," Anna retorted.

"Look, there's no need to start another fight!" Lewis shot back.

"Let's just write down a list of questions in case we might decide to contact them," Anna pled.

"In case we *might* decide? You mean, *when* we contact them," Lewis mumbled, knowing full well of Anna's persistence. Anna, for once, sensed that this was not the time to pursue her idea, but a seed had been planted in her mind.

For the next several weeks she saw the same ad repeated in the paper, and about three weeks later, she broached the subject again.

"Lewis, the ad about that little boy is still here. Would it hurt to just write and see if he's still available?"

"Available?" Lewis thundered. "It's a little boy!" Then, in his most sarcastic voice, he announced, "Hello. Is the hay you have for sale still available? Or how about, I'm writing to inquire whether or not the car you advertised is still available!" Lewis paused to let his words sink in.

"Don't tease me," Anna pouted. "I'm really serious. We've wanted a family, and we can't have any kids of our own. Maybe this is God's way of giving us a family."

Instead of starting yet another argument, Lewis decided to go along with Anna's "crazy idea," just to pacify her. So they spent the next several minutes jotting down questions they would ask *if* they decided to write. "Why is he up for adoption? What's wrong with him? Exactly how old is he? What does he look like? Is he normal in his development? What illnesses has he had? Where is he living? Who is he living with?" They crossed off some questions and added others. When Anna felt that the list included all the most important questions, she sighed contentedly and laid the paper down. She started rocking, humming a little song.

Lewis could sense a lift in Anna's spirits and wondered hopefully if some spring greenery might be poking through her wintry blanket of depression. Although happy about the change in her demeanor, he still hoped she would forget the whole idea.

But Anna didn't forget. She kept turning the idea over in her mind, savoring the thought of a child to hold in her lap. "Lewis, I want to write to them," she declared emphatically one day.

Without a fight, he replied, "OK, it's all right with me."

Anna hurried to the desk. "Dear Lottie," she wrote. "I'm inquiring about whether or not the little boy has been adopted yet."

When her pen finished scratching her signature, she read the letter to Lewis. "And I didn't even mention the word 'available,' either," she snorted when she was through.

Every day Anna hurried out to the mailbox, hoping for a reply. At last, she opened the little door to reveal an envelope from Colorado Springs. Anna tore open the envelope. Her hands trembled as she drew out the white paper. "No, he hasn't yet been adopted," she read. "He's still available. Several others have written, but no one has made any definite plans to even come and see the boy, much less make a decision to adopt him. I don't know why. He's an adorable child."

Anna held her breath a moment, then ran into the house waving the envelope in her hand. "Hurrah!" she shouted into the empty house. "He still hasn't been adopted!" She could hardly wait for Lewis to tap his way home from work.

Lewis wasn't nearly as excited and grew increasingly perturbed as Anna and Lottie exchanged letter after letter. "Not so fast!" he warned one day. "What kind of arrangements do they want?"

"We both have college educations," Anna wrote in the next letter.

"We both work in the church and are solid Christians. The doctor has advised me that I will be unable to bear any children. We would feel honored to raise your little boy for you, but do need to know what kind of arrangements you have in mind." She read the letter to Lewis.

"OK, send it," Lewis growled.

The letter exchange continued, each one seeming to lead to a fight between Lewis and Anna regarding some new detail. Anna kept writing the additional letters Lewis thought needed to be sent.

Back in Colorado Springs, Lottie and Lois had a dilemma. More than 300 people had responded to their ad! "So, how are you going to tell Charles?" Lois asked.

"Well, I guess the time has come to 'cross the bridge,'" Lottie admitted. "I guess we'll just have to come clean with Charles. Let's talk to him together. We could have him come over a few minutes before supper tonight."

"Just sit down for a minute," Lottie said when Charles arrived.

Charles pulled up a chair and sat at the table.

Lois nodded to Lottie, but she shook her head "No, you tell him."

"No! It was your idea!" retorted Lois.

Charles looked from one to the other, bewildered. "What idea?"

There was a long pause. Finally, Lottie spoke. "Charles, we can't take care of Little Charlie any longer," she began. "And besides, it's not fair for him to not have a home. He needs a place of his own. So I—we—well, Lois and I decided to sort of prove the Lord, so we ran an ad in the church paper, and, well, now you have to decide," she finished lamely.

"I have to decide what?"

"Well, here are 300 responses to our ad, and you must decide who would be the best parents for Little Charlie," Lottie explained.

"What ad? Decide *what*? What are you talking about?" Charles asked.

"Well, we advertised that there was a little boy up for adoption and 300 people have responded."

Charles rose from his chair, then slumped back to his seat. "But Little Charlie isn't up for adoption!" he shouted. "You had no right to do that! Just throw all the letters away!" Anger flashed from his eyes like daggers, first toward Lottie, then toward Lois. A dark red color engulfed his face and the veins in his neck bulged. He clenched and unclenched his fists, clenched them again, then pounded the table. He jumped to his feet and stomped toward the door. "How could you do this to me? What in the world were you thinking?" he demanded, his words bouncing wildly off the walls and rattling the windows. He grabbed the doorknob and stormed out. Lottie and Lois chased after him.

"Listen, Charles," Lois pleaded. "Please listen to us. Little Charlie doesn't have a place he can call home. He has had no consistent discipline. He needs that."

Charles just stomped toward his truck.

"Let him cool down, Lottie," Lois counseled. "We can try again to-morrow."

Later that evening, Lottie heard a knock at her door. She had never seen Charles appear so utterly beaten. He seemed even more forlorn than he had looked at Emily's funeral. His shoulders sagged and his eyes were red.

"I've cried and cried," Charles admitted. "How can I deny what you and Lois have said? I went home, and after the kids were in bed, I knelt to pray. All I could see was Little Charlie bouncing from you to Lois to me. It really *isn't* fair to him." His voice broke and he sniffled while wiping a tear from his cheek with the back of his hand. "God seemed to say, 'Charles, I'll help you find a good home for Little Charlie.' So I've come to get the 300 letters. It's breaking my heart, but I guess there's no other way."

Back at home, Charles sorted the letters into three stacks: "No way," "maybe," and "sounds positive." *Who would be the very best parents for Little Charlie?* he wondered. Tearfully, agonizingly, he read and reread the letters. "We need an extra hand around the farm" hit the "no way" stack. "We want a brother for our little boy" were "maybes," but soon Charles eliminated them, too. He gradually narrowed his choice to 10 very posi-tive-sounding letters. Laying these out on his bed, he knelt and prayed as he had never prayed in his life. Tears streamed down his face, blotching the ink on the letters. One by one he eliminated them until he was down to just three letters.

One in particular held Charles' attention. "We both have college ed-ucations," the letter said. "We both work in our local church and are solid Christians. . . . We would feel honored to raise your little boy for you . . ." *Educated. Christians. Can't have their own children. Would feel honored.* This was the letter he finally chose after days of agony. He had never known such pain. How could he give up Little Charlie? Yet how could he deny him a happy and permanent Christian home?

Charles stood at Lottie's door gripping the bundle of 300 letters. "Do what you want with these," he said, handing her all but the one he'd chosen. "My choice is Lewis and Anna Harris." Then he handed her the letter together with the reply he'd written.

Lottie read Charles' letter aloud. "Dear Anna and Lewis. From the 300 people who wrote to me, the Lord has impressed me that you would be the best parents for my precious Little Charlie . . ." As Charles listened, his face grew pale and began to feel that his heart would stop beating at any moment. *What was he doing? But wouldn't this be best for Little Charlie?*

He signed his name, and Lottie posted the letter.

Charles said nothing to any of his children about the possibility of Little Charlie being adopted. Day after day went by with his heart aching continuously. When Lottie told him that Lewis and Anna had responded and were coming to "evaluate the situation," Charles didn't know whether to hope they would or wouldn't like his son.

When Anna received the letter inviting her to come to Colorado Springs, she literally danced for joy. Now she had to convince Lewis! Cajoling, crying, pouting, arguing—Anna tried them all. At last, she wore him down and convinced him to talk with his boss about taking some vacation "to see if maybe we might be interested in thinking about adopting this boy."

Reluctantly, Lewis asked his boss for some vacation time and then visited a local attorney who helped him draw up tentative adoption papers. When Anna saw them, she threw her arms around Lewis and hugged him tightly. "Oh Lewis, at last we will have a family!" she exulted.

Anna swirled into action like a dust storm on the Nebraska prairie. Dawn found her up and dressed with her hair neatly combed. She cleaned the whole house. She cooked "real" meals. No longer sitting listless in her rocking chair for hours, she cleared out the baby clothes from the closet, bought a twin-sized bed at a secondhand store to replace the crib, and made new boyish curtains for the windows.

Spring had arrived!

Chapter 6

ROOTS, NO ROOTS

The last letter, Anna thought as she wrote to advise Lottie and Lois of their arrival time. "Lewis, a week from now, Bradley will be here with us!" she almost sang. "I wonder what the Whites will be like?"

"We'll just go check him out, " Lewis told Anna. "If we like what we see, we'll offer to adopt him."

Anna packed enough lunch for the trip to Colorado and back and bought a few toys she thought a 2 1/2-year-old boy would like.

When the huge wheels on the black train finally ground to a stop at the Colorado Springs station, Lewis reached into his inside coat pocket for the map Lottie had sent and handed it to Anna. "Anna, hail a taxi," he said as she guided him down from the train car.

Moments later Lewis took Anna's arm once again and together they mounted the steps to Lottie's house. Anna took a deep breath and said, "OK Lewis, here we are." Exhaling, she knocked on the door.

"Hello?" Lottie said as she opened the wooden door.

"We're Lewis and Anna Harris," Lewis said, "and, as you know, we've come to possibly adopt your boy—if we like what we see."

"Oh, come in," Lottie invited. "Only I'm not the parent. I'm one of the aunts." She wondered why Lewis held on to Anna's arm as they entered, then noticed him groping to sit on the couch she offered. When she saw the white-tipped cane, she suddenly wondered if this really was the best family for Little Charlie. Too late for changing to another parent now! The Harris' were here!

"If you'll excuse me, I'll go get Charles, Little Charlie's dad. He doesn't have a phone, so it will take a few minutes. He's expecting you, so he should be at home." She slipped out the back door, commenting, "This will give you a chance to get acquainted with Little Charlie."

Little Charlie was playing with a homemade choo-choo train, pushing it around on the floor. Anna looked at his dark hair and blue eyes and felt a twinge of motherliness. Lewis, all business like, wanted to "get it over with as soon as possible" and start back to Lincoln on the afternoon train.

In a few minutes, Lottie and Charles returned.

"Charles, this is Mr. and Mrs. Harris, and folks, this is Charles, Charlie's daddy."

Charles looked at the man staring blankly straight ahead and the woman with the straight back perched on the couch beside him. Then he looked at his son examining his toy train. He clenched and unclenched his fists until they were as tight as his jaw. Something inside him snapped and he shouted, "No! No! I've changed my mind. I'm not letting Little Charlie go." Little Charlie stopped pushing his train and looked from one adult to another.

"But you have to!" Lewis shouted, half rising from his seat. "We've come all the way from Lincoln, Nebraska, because you agreed. Now you're trying to renege. We'll sue you!"

Charles jumped from his chair and started toward Lewis. "You can't sue me," he shouted back. "He's *my* son. I can change my mind if I want to!"

Anna started crying. "All I want is a little boy to love," she wailed.

Lois stood wringing her hands.

"Stop! All of you! Stop this right now!" Lottie finally commanded. "Charles, you sit over here. Anna and Lewis, you stay on the couch. Lois, you sit on that bench. Now listen to me, all of you. Little Charlie deserves a good home. He deserves stability. He deserves some roots. He needs consistency. He needs a Christian mommy and daddy who will love him and train him up in a godly manner. Charles, you can't take care of him. You've tried. Lois and I have tried, and, let's face it, we can't. I snapped at Little Charlie for the thousandth time last night. I've tried, but I've failed. I have no patience with him anymore." Her voice broke, and a tear ran down one cheek. She choked out the next words. "Now if these good people want to take him, what alternative do you have to offer, Charles?"

Silence filled the small house.

Charles sat with his head in his hands, elbows on the table, his voice shaking. "I've lost eight children already. I've lost my precious Emily. What else can you take from me? I've paid for the babysitter during the day. I've paid for his food and bought all his clothes."

"But that's just a start," Lottie said coolly, having regained her composure. "We haven't asked you to pay us for our time, our sleepless nights, our . . ."

Anna felt something stir again. She could be a good mommy. She could provide stability and nurture. So could Lewis. "Listen, folks," Anna said as she leaned forward. "Lewis and I are good people. We go to church every week. We want a family. We will give Little Charlie a good home. We can give him everything you want for him."

All heads turned from Anna to Lewis as he spoke. "He won't be Little Charlie anymore. We'll change his name to Bradley. Our lawyer advises us to arrange a 'no contact' adoption. We'll take Bradley, and you will never hear from him or us again. You must not try to contact us or him. It would be too upsetting for all of us."

More deadly silence. Charles sat as if frozen into stone.

"Well, Charles, what alternative do you have to offer?" Lois asked.

Lois, Lottie, Anna, and Lewis waited. Lewis began tapping his pen on the adoption papers. That and the ticking clock on the mantle were the only sounds in the room. "Here. Just sign this paper, and we'll be on our way," Lewis said. "Then you folks can get your lives back to normal." He held out the adoption papers and his pen toward Charles.

Feeling completely overwhelmed, confused, and helpless, Charles wailed, "Back to normal? *Normal* would be with Emily and Little Charlie and all my other kids. *Normal* would be . . ."

"Yes, but normal isn't reality anymore, Charles," Lois said quietly. "We've tried. We just can't do it any longer."

Little Charlie clung to his daddy, feeling the terrible tension in the room.

Lewis cleared his throat. "Well?"

The four adults all stared at Charles. "It'll be best for Little Charlie, you know," Lottie prompted.

"I can't! Give up my son? Never see him again? No, I can't," Charles shouted. "Never. *Never!*"

"So what do you propose to do?" Anna asked, sounding sympathetic. "We can give him a good, solid home where he can put his roots down and grow into a fine person."

"But never see him again?" Charles agonized.

"That's the way adoptions are done," Lewis said matter-of-factly.

"Charles, just admit that we've failed," Lois said, her voice almost in a whisper. "Just admit that you want something better for Little Charlie. Just let your heart grasp how much better it would be for him to live with Anna and Lewis."

Charles sat weeping, clutching Little Charlie. He groaned, sucked in air, and shook his head. "No."

Minutes passed.

Then, in an agonizing, frantic moment, he grabbed the pen and signed his name.

"Then it's a done deal?" Lewis asked. "This means that you are letting us take him?"

Weeping, Charles nodded his head. "Oh God, help me," was all he could say, all the while clinging to Little Charlie.

"Bradley, come here to Mommy," Anna coaxed.

"No! Not my mommy! No go!" He wrapped his little arms tightly around Charles' neck and wailed loudly.

Lottie pried Little Charlie's arms from Charles' neck and Anna reached over and pulled him from his daddy.

"Charlie, go with this lady. Be a good boy," his daddy managed to choke out the words.

"No! No! No go with you!" Little Charlie screamed. But Anna held firmly to the kicking, screaming little boy. "Lewis, here's my purse. Let's go!"

Lewis tucked the signed paper in his inner suit pocket, took the purse, and held Anna's arm as they walked through the doorway and out to the waiting taxi.

Little Charlie screamed and kicked. Charles started for the door, but Lois and Lottie blocked it. "Let him go," they said. "There's no other way."

"My baby! You just pulled him up by his roots!"

"His roots?" Lois asked. "That's the problem. Little Charlie has no roots. He's been from my house to Lottie's, back to mine, over to yours, back and forth for two and a half years. It's time he *got* some roots somewhere."

Charles put his hands over his ears, partly to shut out Little Charlie's screams, and partly to shut out his sister's words. He collapsed on the couch, held his head in his hands, and wept bitterly.

Chapter 7

ABANDONED AND ABUSED

With one arm guiding Lewis and the other gripping a screaming, kicking, crying Charlie, the three awkwardly climbed the steps onto the black train, already puffing clouds of steam into the azure afternoon sky.

"I no Bradley! I Charlie! I go home!" He struggled to free himself from Anna's firm grip and banged his little fists against the train car's window. Soon he had drained all the strength from his body and fell exhausted on her lap. With each lurch of the train, he would awaken, cry out in fear, then fall back into a fitful sleep.

Somewhere between Colorado Springs and Lincoln, Little Charlie opened his eyes with a start. Stroking his black hair, Anna murmured, "Good boy." Reaching for the lunch bag, she handed him a sandwich.

"Here, Bradley. Eat something," she coaxed.

"I no Bradley! No eat," Little Charlie whimpered groggily, clamping his little mouth shut.

"Stubborn little guy," Lewis observed. "It's not worth the fight, Anna. I can live with the name 'Charles' if you can. We just don't need the 'Little' part."

Reluctantly, Anna agreed. "Here I thought we'd have a little angel to replace our precious Timmy. What a cruel joke!" she whined.

Mile after mile, the train clackety-clacked through golden fields, taking Charlie farther and farther away from all he had known.

"We're home," Anna called as she pushed open the front door. Anna showed Charlie his room, the new teddy bear waiting for him, and the rest of the house. She hugged him and said, "Mommy is so happy to have a little boy to love!"

That was the first—and last—time Anna ever told Charlie she loved him!

He liked having his very own room and bed, and he played with the teddy bear, sometimes crying into its fur. He missed Aunt Lottie, Aunt Lois, his brothers and sister—and especially his daddy.

Mealtime meant war and the table was the battlefield. "Charles no like!" he screamed, only to be told, "Things are different now, Charles. Whether you like it or not, you *will* sit here at the table and eat. Either you eat this or you go hungry," Lewis growled.

"I not eat," he replied.

"OK, you can get down. When you are hungry, you will eat what you are served."

Lewis returned to his work at the Christian Record, assuming that in time Charles would fit neatly into their family and fill the aching void in their hearts.

"Lewis, I'm so disappointed in Charles," Anna wept each night. "I dreamed of the perfect child to replace my precious Timmy, but Charles is *far* from perfect! Maybe we should send him back," Anna said, sounding defeated.

"Let's give him a while, Anna. He'll settle down. Just think how you'd feel if you'd been taken from everything familiar and everyone you knew. Just give him some time," Lewis advised.

And Charlie did begin to "settle down." He learned to call this strange lady mommy, and this big man daddy. It didn't take many days for him to realize that he was living under different rules, different discipline. Even though Aunt Lottie and Aunt Lois didn't always have time to read him a bedtime story and say prayers with him, most of the time they did. When Anna said, "Go to bed, Charles. Wash your face and brush your teeth," he asked for a story.

"Bedtime story?" Jesus story?" he queried.

"No! Just go to bed and go to sleep."

"Pray with me?"

Silence. After a while, memories of bedtime Bible stories faded.

Anna never rocked Charlie or even picked him up. Lewis worked long hours and was rarely around to play with him, tell him a story, or even pat him on the head. He played with his toys alone. How he longed for a hug, a kiss, or an "I love you." He waited in vain. Whatever mothering instincts Anna thought she would have when she envisioned adopting Charlie vanished with her fading dream of the perfect child to replace the one she lost. Temper tantrums grew fewer and fewer as Charlie retreated into his silent world of aloneness. For Anna, the dream boy she had longed for died and she was left with a burden, not a son.

Mercifully, Charlie remembered little about past Christmas seasons. He watched—and waited—for an invitation to help while Anna decorated the little Christmas tree in the corner of the front room. Now 3 years old, he tried to talk about "presents" and "Kissmass."

"No presents for you. Too poor," Anna told him gruffly as she placed the last candle on a green bough.

Christmas day dawned bright and clear, the sun reflecting off the newly fallen three inches of snow.

"Play in snow? Me go play in snow," Charlie grinned.

"No. It's too cold."

His smile melted, and he pressed his nose against the window to watch the children next door. They looked about his age and were sure having fun, laughing and whooping as they made a snowman with their daddy's help. Charlie's eyes followed them as they fell backward into the powder and made snow angels and tramped out a circle for playing tag.

"Me go play with them?" he pled.

"No! Too cold!"

Throwing himself on the floor, he kicked and screamed, begging to go play in the snow.

"For the last time, *no*! And because you are such a naughty boy, you won't get any Christmas presents at all!" Unbelievingly, Charles watched as Anna removed his one package from under the tree and took it away.

After dinner Lewis and Anna exchanged a few gifts, and true to her word, Charlie did not receive even one present. That night Charles cried himself to sleep, his little arms locked around his teddy bear.

When Charles was about 5 years old, something happened to totally change his life.

"Lewis," Anna ventured one day, "I think I'm pregnant."

"Impossible," Lewis snorted. "The doctor told you that you'd never be able to bear another child."

"I know, and I haven't had a day of morning sickness, but I'm gaining weight, and I think I felt movement last night."

"Impossible!" Lewis repeated.

But Anna continued to gain weight, and when she was sure she was feeling the baby move, she took herself to the doctor.

"Well, I never," Dr. Wiggins said after he'd carefully examined Anna. "I never!"

"You never what?" Anna demanded.

"I never thought you could get pregnant again. But congratulations! Near as I can tell, in about four months, you'll be a proud mama again!"

Anna nearly floated home. Another baby! What could be more wonderful?

"Lewis, we need to make Charles' room ready for our baby," Anna announced the next day.

"But what about Charles?" Lewis protested.

"Well, we have a big attic. We can put a bed up there for him," she replied firmly.

Lewis leaned a ladder against the wall below the opening in the hall ceiling. Bewildered Charlie stood with head back and mouth open watching two hired men hang a light on a wire in the attic, then shove his mattress and springs up through the hole in the ceiling.

"Anna, could you climb up the ladder and help Charles make his bed?" Lewis called as the hired men left.

"No way!" Anna screeched. "I'd fall and that would be the death of me and our baby!"

"Ah, come on," Lewis pleaded. "You aren't that big or unsteady yet."

"So you want to risk my falling and losing our baby?" Anna screamed. "You may not want this baby, but I do, and there is *no way* I'm climbing that ladder!"

Confused, Charlie placed his right hand on a crosspiece of the rough wooden ladder, then a foot on the lowest rung. When his head appeared above the hole in the ceiling, he looked around. His mattress and bedsprings sat alone in the middle of nowhere and looked as lonely and rejected as he felt. No windows, no pictures on the wall. He couldn't figure out what he'd done to deserve this. He cried himself to sleep every night for several weeks, alone in his dark attic room.

At first a place of rejection and fear, his attic cave morphed into a place of safety for him. Here, Anna couldn't get at him, and she didn't holler at him quite as often.

True to the doctor's word, Benjamin Lewis Harris arrived, a squalling, red fighter. From her first view of him, Anna loved him fiercely, and Lewis shared her admiration and love for their son.

"Mommy loves her little boy," Anna crooned while Charlie stood off to one side. "Tickle, tickle, tickle," she'd laugh as she blew on Benji's tummy. "Rock-a-bye baby," she'd sing while she rocked back and forth, back and forth. For what seemed hours on end, Charles would stand, forlorn, watching Mommy and Benji bonding.

Christmas that year was something else. Benjamin's many packages stacked one on top of another under the Christmas tree. "Anna, this one's for you, from Benjamin," Lewis said. "And here's one to me from Benji. Ho, ho, ho! And here's another for Benjamin from Santa. And Grandma sent one for Benji. Ho ho ho!"

Charles waited until his heart nearly broke. There were no presents under the tree for him. He got an orange and some socks, but they weren't wrapped neatly in sparkly paper like the other gifts. They were in the shopping bag from the store. Not even one real present! Something wasn't right!

When little Mary Ann arrived about a year and a half later, Anna's joy seemed complete. Benji and Mary Ann lacked for nothing.

A year later, Lewis arrived home from work with a package under his arm. "Happy birthday! Here's a pretty dress for my precious Mary Ann," he crooned. "And here's a new rocking horse for Benji. We didn't want you to feel left out," Daddy explained.

But no one seemed to even notice Charlie, once again standing alone in the shadows, watching, waiting, longing.

One afternoon, Anna's shrill voice echoed through the house. "Charles, stop that!" she yelled. "Can't you ever do anything right? Lewis, come here and get Charles," Anna called to her husband. "He just stomped across my mopped floor!"

Father's chair creaked as he rose from it. "Charles, come here!" he commanded.

Charlie knew that if he went to his father, he'd have to walk across the floor again, but he responded, "I'm coming, Dad."

"Get off my floor!" Anna screamed as he started toward Lewis.

"Oh shut up, Anna," Lewis shouted. "How can he come unless he walks across your stupid floor?"

"Don't yell at me," she shouted.

"I'm going to the attic," Charles said as he passed Lewis, touching him so Lewis knew he had come.

Lewis turned and followed Charlie. "Always crabbing about something, she is," he mumbled. "If it isn't this, it's that. And if isn't that, then it's something else."

Half an hour later, Charlie heard Anna yelling again, "Charles come here!"

"Yes," he answered as he scrambled down the ladder.

"Charles, go get some more firewood. Do I have to tell you every move to make? Look at the firewood box. Empty—again! Can't you think for yourself? What kind of a no-good kid are you, anyway? You'll never amount to anything."

Charlie shut the door behind himself, hoping to shut out her stream of accusations.

Short for his age and not as strong as most kids, it was sometimes hard for him to breathe. Yet, he piled on as many sticks of wood as he could manage and went back inside, dumping the wood in the wood box.

"You stupid kid. Can't you ever do anything right? Line those sticks up even and straight. And look at what a he-man you are! All of five or six sticks of wood! We should call you Samson," she jeered. "Nope—you'll never amount to a hill of beans!"

Silently, Charles tiptoed out of the kitchen and retreated to his attic room. Her voice followed him up the ladder.

Charles sat on the edge of his bed, not knowing how to feel. *You no-good kid . . . you'll never amount to anything.* The thoughts swirled in his head like a merry-go-round that never stopped. *I guess I am stupid after all. Yep, I'm stupid . . . no! I don't want to be stupid! What am I supposed to do? I wish I could figure this out.*

I wanted to scream, to slap my "mother" in the face. I wanted to rant and rave at her, at the world, at everything. I admitted that I hated—yes, I hated my mother! I wanted to run away, to just leave this horrible situation.

As I sat there on the edge of a lumpy mattress staring into the darkness of a cold attic, a very grown-up thought rose slowly in my mind, like the morning sun beginning to splash thawing rays on a frosty landscape. Maybe I was not stupid, as my mother labeled me, and, even more, maybe I didn't have to agree with her bitter predictions about me. Maybe my life was not about "he" or "him," but about "me" and "my." Maybe the thoughts racing in my mind were my thoughts—not anyone else's. Maybe I was in charge of me—no one else—and maybe life would become what I would make of it.

Chapter 8

MY FIRST JOB

It was already dark when Mother started in on me again one evening at the supper table. "Charles, the wood bin is nearly empty again. When will you *ever* notice!"

"Oh, shut up, Anna," Lewis grunted. "Leave the kid alone."

"Charles," 4-year-old Benji piped up, "Mommy said you didn't carry in enough wood to last through the night. Now I'll freeze to death tonight."

"No you won't," I growled. "I'll go get some more right now."

"But I thought you were afraid of the dark," Mother taunted.

I'm not as afraid of the dark as I am sick and tired of all you guys yelling at me, I thought, knowing I didn't dare speak the words. Stomping from the table, I slammed the door behind me. I wanted to stomp and slam doors unendingly! Life simply wasn't fair.

Benji and Mary Ann thrived under their parents' attention and care. I felt like I was dying inside. I had discovered that the school library had books I could check out, so I retreated more and more to the attic. Sitting on my mattress under the single light bulb, my eyes eagerly scanned page after page. Among those black letters I discovered a fantasyland where everything was perfect, a place where I was loved and wanted. My attic became my sanctuary.

But Mother's shrill voice could penetrate my sanctuary, and I dared not ignore it after the pitch rose to a certain decibel! I learned to calculate pretty well how long I could remain upstairs.

"Charles, get down here right now and scrub this kitchen floor," or, "Charles, come here and do the dishes," or any one of a dozen other chores. I knew now that my chief function in the home was "chore boy"—or slave! I was allowed to eat with the family, and I always had enough, but there was absolutely no love, no nurturing from Mother.

"Charles, can you walk with me to the office?" Lewis asked one day. Thus began a daily ritual, and those walks created a bond between us. Soon, I *felt* like calling him Dad. I *had* to call Anna Mother, but in my heart I never fully accepted her as my mother.

Every week found me at church with the family. Mother taught a Sabbath school class for 3- to 5-year-olds, and Dad taught a large class for adults. Even though he was totally blind, his class was always one of the most popular ones in the large church. For the church service, my younger brother, sister, and I sat together with Dad and Mother about two thirds of the way back from the pulpit, and always near the center aisle. But it seemed that we never took our religion home; it stayed in that large church building, waiting for us to showcase once a week.

One lovely spring Sunday, when I was about 10 years old, a neighbor lady knocked on the front door and asked if I could come and dig out all the dandelion weeds from her front lawn.

"Are you sure you want Charles to do that?" Mother asked, drying a kettle as she walked from the kitchen. "He probably won't know how, or he'll miss half of them. Stupid kid," she added under her breath.

"Yes, I want Charles to help me," she countered. "I'll teach him how, and I think he'll do just fine."

I didn't know what to think. Here was a woman who thought I could do something! I listened carefully as she knelt on the lawn and told me what to do: "You use this little tool. Slide it into the ground right where all the leaves clump together. See that little fork at the end of the metal blade? That goes around the root, and then, when you push the handle toward the ground, the leverage pulls the weed out. It isn't too difficult, and the recent rain has made the ground good and soft."

I listened attentively, and as I tried it with her watching, she approved, saying, "Good job, Charles. That's the way. Now, I know there are lots of dandelions, so just take your time, and try to get the roots out on all of them."

I would have climbed to the top of the highest mountain to prove to her that I could be trusted. As the sun rose higher, I began to feel beads of sweat under my straw hat, but I kept at it. She'd given me a box to put the weeds in, and the pile of weeds inside grew bigger and bigger.

When I was about half finished with the lawn, the weed box was full. I dashed home for a quick sandwich while Mother was gone somewhere. Returning to the neighbor's house, I knocked on her front door, holding out the box. "Ma'am," I said, "the box is full, but I still have about half of your front lawn to do."

She seemed genuinely pleased, and she praised me, "What a great job, Charles! I knew you could do it! Here, let's empty the box into the garbage bin, and then if you want to, you can keep working."

It was now officially hot, and I really didn't want to keep working, but at the same time I *did* want to! She liked my work! What a thrill to hear a few encouraging words!

I worked most of the day on her lawn, and before I knocked again, I checked to be sure I'd gotten every weed. She came out and inspected the lawn with me again. "Good job, Charles! Great work!" She handed me two silver dollars and said, "You earned every bit of this. You are a good worker."

I nearly floated home, but as soon as I opened the back door and came into the kitchen, Mother started in. "Well, how come you quit so soon?" she asked.

So soon! I thought. *I worked all day on that lawn, and I didn't quit until every last dandelion was gone.* But I didn't argue. I simply said, "I finished the job."

"And I'll bet half the weeds are still there," she chided. "Can't you ever do a good job of anything?"

"She told me I did a great job, and she paid me two silver dollars for the work," I said quietly.

"She *what?*"

I repeated what I'd said and held out the two silver dollars for her to see.

"Well, you owe me one of those dollars to help pay for your food," she said as she snatched one of coins from my hand.

My eyes grew wide, my jaw clenched, and I felt my face flush with anger. But Dad had taught me to be respectful, so I simply turned from her, climbed up the ladder to the attic, and sat steaming on the edge of my bed. *How could I owe her for my food?* I wondered. *Why didn't she praise me like the neighbor lady did?*

When I was 13, Dad got me a job in a little one-man print shop. I oiled presses and cleaned out the papers. Once in a while, the owner would let me stand on a box and feed the press. Little did I know then how valuable that small job would prove to be someday. But God knew—and He was already preparing me for my future.

I picked up other odd jobs, mowing lawns, raking yards, even cleaning trash from a vacant lot so it would be safe for the neighborhood kids to play there. Mother took half of everything I earned. I don't know if Dad ever found out about it or not.

One day while walking around downtown, I saw a "Help Wanted" sign in the window of Smith Brothers Ice Cream Shop. The bell hanging by a string on the door tinkled as I stepped onto the black and white checkerboard floor. A few minutes later I left, the newest part-time employee. The ice cream shop was about five miles from the print shop, and I knew I would need a bicycle to get to my jobs on time.

The methodical roar of the printing press filled the little shop when I walked in and up to my boss at the press. I shouted, "Sir, could you loan me $20 to buy a bike?"

"A bicycle, eh?" he replied. "Sure. We can deduct a bit from each of your paychecks until it's all repaid."

The tires on that old second-hand bike should have blown and the frame should have fallen apart, but Someone knew my needs and held that bicycle together for me.

Chapter 9

REBELLION

Entering my teen years, I began to see very clearly the differences between what I heard in church and what was practiced in our home. Except for Dad saying grace at the evening meal, which consisted of the same three or four short sentences every time, I cannot recall praying or studying the Bible as a family even once. Our diet differed radically from what we knew and believed the Bible taught about healthful eating. Breakfast was ham and eggs some mornings and bacon and eggs others. We consumed an inordinate amount of sweets, which did nothing to help my dad's expanding figure. Hot dogs appeared regularly for supper, but I never questioned Mother about why we ate the very foods that were pronounced unclean at church.

Our home was the scene of almost constant bickering, quarrelling, and loud arguments. I would retreat to my attic sanctuary, or, if the weather was good, I'd go outside just to get away from the continual hassle. I began to spend more time at work.

I was one of the carhops at the ice cream shop. I would go out to the customer's car, take the order, bring it in to the cook, and then deliver it when the meal was ready. Carhopping began to poke through my timid demeanor. I felt a new confidence begin to surge through me, and soon I was able to smile and even make light conversation with customers, which also brought me some pretty nice tips. Another good thing about working there was that I could eat whatever I wanted from the menu.

I started skipping church more and more. Sometimes Dad would chide, "Charles, you need to come to church with us," but I could see no reason for attending. It didn't seem to do anything for Mother and Dad's everyday life, even though they enjoyed their weekly status as pillars of the church. I knew better! Why would I want to become like that?

The College View Academy I attended also began to be a joke to me. Dad had insisted that I attend a church school and get a Christian education; a much less expensive public high school was simply out of the question in his mind. However, I began to inwardly scoff at the Seventh-day

Adventist religion the school promoted simply because it wore the same name as that of my hypocritical parents. Since I was working two jobs, I was making pretty decent money for someone my age. Religiously and practically, who needed school? But I was not about to challenge Dad on the subject, so I kept attending.

One beautiful spring day, my classmates and I had a hard time quieting down after the lunch break. The daffodils and forsythia were in full bloom, and the sky was such a deep, clear blue that it seemed close enough to touch. A warm, gentle breeze blew, which after the cold winter was most inviting. We all had spring fever, and the balmy day awakened restlessness in our very bones!

"Class, settle down," Miss Perkins commanded. I expect you to behave as the 10th graders you are." Just about the time silence finally reigned, a knock at the door arrested everyone's attention. The school secretary stuck her head in the door. "Miss Perkins, please send Charles Harris to the office immediately." She spoke the words so loudly that everyone could hear. All eyes turned from the doorway to me.

Why me? I wondered. *What have I done?* I couldn't think of any reason why I should be called to the principal's office. Bewildered, I walked down the hall in a daze. The principal met me at the door to his office. "Charles," he said, "your father has become very ill. You need to go home immediately." Your mother just called and asked me to send you home. Don't take time to get your books or sweater. Hurry!"

My heart skipped several beats. Big, strong, healthy Dad—sick? I dashed out the door and covered the four blocks to the house in record time. It was far enough to give my mind the opportunity to develop a chant in rhythm with my footsteps. *Dad's sick, I'm scared, Dad's sick, I'm scared.* The words pounded in my brain.

Bursting through the front door, I skidded to an abrupt stop. A hospital bed had been moved into the parlor, and Dad lay struggling for breath. I could hear the gurgling from clear across the room. His skin looked awful! Dark, purple-red blotches covered his face, but his arms and hands almost matched the white sheets. The left side of his face drooped, and saliva dribbled from his mouth. Two men were working over him. One of them, Dr. Howell, listened to Dad's chest with his stethoscope, straightened, and slowly shook his head, "No." Then he turned to the other man. "Nurse, check his pulse and blood pressure again."

I started toward Dad. "No Charles!" Mother barked. "There's nothing you can do. Don't go near the bed. Just go on to your work."

Why in the world did you call me home? I asked her in my mind. I longed to just sit and hold Dad's hand, but Mother stood between us, her mouth set in a grim, hard line. There was nothing I could do but leave Dad and go to my afternoon print shop job, to be followed later by my evening job at the ice cream shop. Despite nearly round-the-clock care, Dad died a couple of days later. "Massive stroke" meant little to my 15-year-old brain. All I knew was that my dad was gone.

It seemed that my world had ended! Even though he was usually distant and very demanding, I felt I could trust Dad. Sometimes we would talk briefly about the concerns on my heart. About a year before, some of the kids at school, and a girl named Susie in particular, had begun taunting me, "You're adopted, you're adopted."

I had rushed home and asked Mother, "Am I adopted?"

Mom's face grew red and her eyes flashed. She slapped my face so hard I went sprawling across the kitchen floor. "Don't you ever mention such a lie again. Of course it's not true! Who told you such a thing?"

"Susie," I replied.

"Well, Susie is a liar! She doesn't know a thing. Don't you ever talk about it again!

Needless to say, I never breathed another word to Mother about it! But Susie kept on.

Several months later, I had been walking Dad to work one morning when I ventured, "I was thinking, if I was adopted, maybe that's the reason Mother doesn't like me."

Dad had stopped walking abruptly. I'd been holding his arm as I always did as his guide. He turned toward me and stood silently on the sidewalk for what seemed like hours. Then, with a low, halting, almost choking voice he said, "Your mother and I both love you, son. Don't ever forget that! But for now, I want you to promise me that you will never say anything about this to anyone again. When the time comes, when you are a bit older, I'll tell you all about it."

And now Dad was gone! Who could I talk to now? Who could I ask?

I had never been to a funeral before. The organ played horribly depressing music, and I wished they'd turn on some more lights. I could feel death pressing in on me. After the speeches, songs, and eulogy, people got up and walked past the casket. I'd never seen a dead body lying in a coffin, and looking down at Dad's pale face unnerved me. He wore his best suit and tie. How they got the splotches off his face I'll never know, but his skin looked a sickly, pasty white. A stupid grin forced his lips up in a way I'd never seen them before. The whole experience haunted me for years.

I'd learned long ago not to ask Mother questions, and the only person on earth I trusted lay under the sod! *Dad, why did you leave me? What am I supposed to do now?* I wondered.

I returned to school but couldn't concentrate. My whole world had collapsed. Mother and I grew more and more distant, if that were possible. I felt sure she deliberately tried to avoid me.

But fate kindly unraveled only one portion of my life at a time.

About three somber weeks later, I returned home from school and noticed some of my clothes piled on a rickety table on the porch. I parked my bike, walked up the three steps with my eyes fastened on the clothes pile, and saw a box sitting beside. In it were the rest of my clothes. A note stuck out from beneath a pair of trousers.

"I have taken care of you for the past 12 years and am no longer able to do it. Take your clothes and do not return. You are no longer welcome here." There was no signature, no greeting. Just a cold, abrupt note. It seemed that Mother wanted to force me away from everything that might represent Dad and security.

Why 12 years? I'm 15! Was Susie right? Right then I made a decision: *I'll never call you Mom or Mother again!*

Stunned, hurt, confused, and angry, I tore the note into tiny bits and threw them at the front door. After enduring the violence from my hand, they scattered and floated downward, some slipping to freedom between the worn, wooden boards of the porch. *Just like me,* I thought. *Thrown out violently, but now I'm free—free from her!* I had two jobs, and even with Anna taking half of everything I earned, I had been paying my own tuition for months and buying my own clothes. This place offered me only somewhere to eat and sleep. I didn't need her—I could take care of myself!

I grabbed the box and pile of clothes, yanked a piece of rope from a peg, and lashed the box to my bicycle rack. Stuffing the rest of my clothes under my arm, I pedaled toward the home of a school friend, Jake. He and I were as close as I would allow anyone to be.

Jake's mother greeted me at the door. "Oh, Charles, do come in!" she invited. She seemed to be expecting me. She had kindly invited me to stay with her family several times since Dad died, and it became clear that she knew more about my situation at home than I had thought.

One afternoon, Jake's mother startled me with a question. "Charles, why don't you just make our house your permanent home?"

I was too stunned to answer for a moment. Scenes of Anna's cruel attitude flashed in my mind. Even though Jake's mother and father had been kind, my mind warned, *Don't trust anyone. They'll just hurt you.* I could feel bitterness rising in my throat. I could almost taste it!

"No, ma'am," I said. "I thank you, but I can't. I mean, I don't want . . . um, I mean, I want freedom . . . um, no . . . I just can't," I mumbled. Anna's continual rejection, Dad's untimely death, and my lack of ability to make friends were seeds pushed deep into the rocky soil of my heart that grew into ugly weeds of stubbornness, rebellion, and distrust of anyone—even someone who was trustworthy. Checking the local newspaper, I found a furnished room where I could be totally independent.

I would occasionally attend church, and on one such occasion, not wanting to sit anywhere near Anna and my two younger siblings, I chose a vacant seat behind three saintly old women. One by one they craned their necks and stared at me. Then I heard one of them say, "Well, what do you know? Charles Harris is here. He'll never amount to anything. I can't imagine why he wastes his time coming to church." And they puffed themselves up haughtily.

Indeed, I thought. *Why should I waste my time here?*

I left church at the end of the service and spent two miserable hours in my room. Raised in the belief that sundown on Friday to sundown on Saturday was the Sabbath and that no work should be done during those hours, I began to think about my options. *What's the use of keeping the Sabbath? Since I'm probably going to hell anyway, I might as well work every night.* One of the perks of working at Smith Brothers was that employees could eat all they wanted for free. *If I do that, I'd get a free supper every day of the week!*

I rode my bike the familiar route to Smith Brothers Ice Cream and approached my boss who was repairing one of the machines. "Sir," I said, "Can I start working every night? I need a few extra shekels to pay my room rent."

"Sure, Charles, we could use some extra help," he replied. "And remember that you can eat as much as you want here." From 6:00 in the evening till 2:00 in the morning, I handed out scoops of ice cream. And somewhere among all that chocolate and vanilla went my church attendance and prayer.

A year passed. I survived mostly by eating all I could at the ice cream shop—milkshakes, banana splits, sundaes, chili, hamburgers, and more ice cream. I couldn't afford to buy food, so what I ate there usually had to last me until I returned the next evening!

Although my teachers must have known something about my situation, only one ever asked how I was dealing with my dad's death; only one showed any personal interest at all. What a treat it would have been to be invited home to dinner once in a while, or have someone take a personal interest in me. But such was not to be.

While I never drank alcohol or tried smoking, which I considered to be dirty habits that I couldn't afford anyway, I did begin using foul language and gambling with my tip money. I became quite clever at my bets, usually coming out the winner.

To retreat from the jagged edges of reality, I started reading thriller novels, and in time, I admitted even to myself that these stories had become an addiction. I knew Dad would be displeased if he knew the way I was living, but he had abandoned me, so why should I care?

Even though Anna lived no more than a few blocks from where I'd found a room, I never went to see her, and she never tried to look me up. My hatred for her grew more intense, and along with it grew bitterness toward her church and her God.

Chapter 10

A VOICE IN THE NIGHT

At the end of my junior year of high school I was still working two jobs in addition to school and was living almost entirely on ice cream shop food. How I ever maintained an acceptable grade point average was a miracle, because the only time I had to study was if things were quiet at the ice cream shop—and they seldom were.

In the tiny cracks of time between school and work I lost myself in cheap novels from the local library, burning the precious little time I had to develop and nurture friendships. I grew more and more lonely and more and more bitter.

Every day, as soon as school was out, I'd hop on my trusty bike and ride the five miles to the print shop, where I'd work until 5:30 or 6:00. Then I'd pedal to the ice cream shop where I'd hurriedly change clothes and work until 2:00 the next morning. I'd ride home exhausted, crash into bed, only to cringe at the sound of the alarm clock waking me to get ready for school.

After work one night, as I pedaled my bicycle toward home, I had to pass through a grove of trees. The poorly lighted street cast eerie shadows, and a stretch of about half a mile extended ahead of me where there were no homes or businesses. The whole scene looked haunted to my blinking, bleary eyes.

As I rolled into the grove of trees, it seemed I heard someone calling, "Charles!"

I pedaled faster, my heart beating wildly. Again I heard my name coming from the thick stand of trees that lined both sides of the street. The voice startled me, and I tried to push my tired body to pedal faster. When the voice called the third time, my fear mysteriously dissolved into a warm feeling that washed over me. Squeezing the brake lever, I put a foot on the ground and stood there in near total darkness.

Propelled by a mysterious power, I pushed my bike into the trees, sensing that God Himself was calling me. A deep impression said to me, "This is your very last chance before eternity."

What was happening? Was God telling me I was about to die? My father's pasty white face lying in the casket flooded my mind. All my bitterness and bad habits came up before me like a thick, black cloud. I felt almost as if I were about to die that very night.

"God, can You forgive me for all my sinful, rebellious ways?" I prayed aloud, dropping to my knees on the damp grass. I prayed and wept for some time, having done neither for a long time. I'd learned the basics of prayer in my childhood Sabbath school classes at church but had never grasped the real power of prayer. A Bible verse I had been expected to memorize as a child began playing and replaying in my mind: "I have loved thee with an everlasting love: therefore, with lovingkindness have I drawn thee" (Jeremiah 31:3). That night, there in the grove of trees, I felt God drawing me to His love while an unfamiliar peace hugged me close. I felt God accepting me just the way I was!

Thinking I should say something in return, but not knowing exactly what, I stumbled, "God, help me to make myself good." It was an awkward, misdirected request, but God knew it was my heart's sincere response to Him. The tree grove experience was my turning point, and I carried it with me the rest of my life.

I immediately set off to change my behavior, to get back to the religion of my childhood. The very next day, I screwed up my courage for a talk with my boss. "Sir, some things have changed. I was wondering if I could have every Friday night off?" Surely God must have been seeking to encourage me and strengthen my feeble faith, because the boss said, "Sure, Charles. No problem."

I began to feel convicted that the thriller novels I was reading didn't promote Christian growth, and I decided I would try exchanging them for the Bible. Back then, the King James Version was the only version I knew anything about. It was the Bible of my childhood, and I read it every day. However, because of its antiquated English, my teenage mind could handle only a couple of minutes at a time.

Starting in the New Testament, I began to see Jesus as the Son of God and as a real person—someone with whom I could relate. It became more and more apparent that He loved me—Charles Harris! I started going back to church too. My life didn't immediately turn around, but God had my attention.

Chapter 11

GRADUATION

Graduation from high school! The sky had changed from clear and blue to blotchy and gray, and dark clouds threatened to dump their load on the graduates. We were all lined up, waiting to march into the gymnasium. I stood with the rest of my classmates, alternately scanning the sky and hugging myself against the chill wind.

Here I was, graduating! *I never thought I'd make it,* I thought to myself. In spite of having to work at the print shop, and at the ice cream shop, I had managed to complete all the requirements for graduation. Granted, I'd squeaked by some classes with a "D," but I had a "C" average.

I yawned. Last night's work had been busier than usual, and I hadn't dropped off to sleep until 3:00 in the morning. The other grads were chatting, joking, and in great spirits. I stood alone, with space both ahead of and behind me in the line. *Still a loner. Always a loner,* I thought to myself. *I never know what to say.*

"Hey Charles, where are your family and friends sitting?" someone yelled. The question was intended to hurt, and it did.

"What family? You know the answer," I mumbled bitterly. The pain stabbed my heart. *No family. No friends. And everybody knows it. What was there to celebrate?*

Strains of "Pomp and Circumstance" pealed majestically through the open doors, and the line of graduates began slowly moving inside. The last graduate marched into the gym just as raindrops started pelting the building. Music. Speeches. Tributes to parents. Finally, it was time for the diplomas to be awarded to each student.

"Janie Jones, Valedictorian," announced the registrar. Shrill whistles, cheers, clapping, and foot stomping erupted.

"Peter Willis, Salutatorian." It sounded like he had an entire cheering section.

Then began the alphabetical order of the remaining graduates. Anderson, Bailey, Cole . . .

Each name called elicited at least a few claps or cheers.

"Charles Harris," called the registrar. Silence broke the rhythm. No cheers, no clapping. The silence gripped my heart as I moved forward to claim my diploma. Like an automaton, I reached out my left hand, grasped the diploma, and gave a slight handshake before I walked off the stage.

I carried my sorrow like the dense clouds outside. I was too emotionless to cry. *Is there no one—no one who cares? What's the use of pursuing an education anyway? What's the meaning of life? Why am I here? What am I supposed to do for the time I walk on this planet? Maybe I should just slip back into the rebellious, wild life I led before that night in the grove.* The monologue inside my head heightened my sense of being alone.

When the ceremony was over, I stood mechanically with the rest of my class and marched outside. The storm had blown over, and the sun was playing hide and seek with some scattered clouds. But the storm still raged on in my head. With no one to celebrate my graduation, why hang around? Quickly and silently, I withdrew from the scene.

I hurriedly exchanged my graduation gown for my printing clothes and peddled my bike down to the print shop to bury myself in work. I knew how to work. But today the ache in my heart felt heavier than it had for years. If only there was someone—anyone—I could talk to, someone with whom I could share my graduation!

As I had begun to do since my experience in the grove, I prayed while working the machines. *God, right now, I'm glad I graduated. Thank you for helping me do that. But Lord, it would have been so much more meaningful if only . . . if only . . . I just feel so alone and left out. I feel like a nobody. Is Anna still haunting me?*

Suddenly I was back sitting on the edge of that lumpy mattress under the light bulb, Anna's shrill voice filtering up the ladder into the attic. *Lord, you told me way back then that I did not have to live by her pronouncements about me and her predictions about my future. You told me that my life was my own to create. Now you're telling me that Jesus was there clapping for me when I was up on that stage—when nobody else was.*

God was meeting each of my needs! With relief bubbling up in my mind, I decided that if He valued me enough to meet these specific needs, He would also guide me along the path that lay ahead.

Chapter 12

UNION COLLEGE FRESHMAN

I wish I could say that my life completely turned around immediately after the grove experience, but because I was trying to make myself good, it was slow going. Swear words would escape my lips almost unconsciously and I was still struggling with the novel reading. Although knowing that gambling was wrong for some time, it was a struggle to give up because I almost always won! No matter how hard I tried, I just couldn't seem to push these habits out of my life. Trying harder was not working.

Then there was the bitter attitude that ate at me. One morning I was reading my Bible when Ephesians 4:31 leaped off the page and into my heart. "Let all bitterness . . . be put away from you." The marginal reference cited Hebrews 12:15, so I turned there and read, ". . . lest any root of bitterness springing up trouble you." God impressed me with the futility of continuing to cherish such hateful feelings in my heart.

How, Lord, I prayed, *can I get rid of the bitter feelings I still have toward Anna, Benji, and Mary Ann? I especially hate Anna, Lord. She's the cruelest, meanest, most hateful person I've ever known. I'm afraid I might even become like her! How can I get rid of my bitterness?*

Quietly listening, I heard God speak through my thoughts. *Remember that unknown author's advice you had to memorize for English class? You know, "Live simply. Love generously. Care deeply. Speak kindly. Leave the rest to God." Right now you can't love or care for someone, but you can live simply and leave the rest to Me. I'll give you someone to love generously, someone to care deeply about—when it's time. You're not ready for that just now. Trust Me, Charles. Let Me remove your bitterness.*

It slowly dawned on me that I couldn't make myself good. It was impossible! But if I would give it to God, He could do it.

OK, God, I said. *I give You my bitter attitude. Please take it away.* Gradually, I gave God more and more of my feelings of hatefulness.

When the print shop offered to raise my salary and give me more hours of work, I sadly said goodbye to my friends at the ice cream shop. I could make more money at printing, even with having to buy food for myself.

As the leaves began to turn their fluorescent yellow and flaming red, I felt impressed that God wanted me to become a minister. *Me? A preacher? I thought. Ridiculous! I can't even talk without stammering!* But I couldn't shake the conviction, so when college registration opened, I fell into line with a bunch of other equally confused freshmen at Union College in Lincoln, Nebraska. Declared major: theology!

I also applied for and got a job at the College Press, thanks to my experience at the commercial print shop the past several years. The two printing jobs made my working hours unbearably long. Between working at the two jobs, attending classes, and trying to find time to study, I had very little time for anything else. But still feeling compelled to *do* various things to "make myself good," I joined a singing band that sang to the residents of a local nursing home each week. I also joined my friend Marty in preaching at a boys' reform school nearby.

Marty exuded happiness. Able to talk on the spur of the moment, he seemed to be a silver-tongued orator. He preached, and my part was to pray. While preaching seemed utterly impossible, praying out loud in front of a group of hardened young men felt almost as intimidating. The boys were a captive audience with no option other than to sit while Marty and I "practiced." I have no idea whether any of them ever accepted Jesus as their Savior, but as I listened to Marty's simple explanations of the gospel and the plan of salvation, God used Marty to help *me* grow.

But something was wrong with me physically. I began to feel more and more tired. My energy level dropped to near zero. Somehow I kept dragging myself to work and classes, but I continued to feel worse and worse. My head pounded, and my head burned with a high fever.

Finally I picked up the phone and called a medical office. "I need to see the doctor," I blurted to the person who answered. "I am really sick, and don't have a clue what's the matter with me."

The lady replied, "Well, it happens that we just had someone call and cancel their appointment for 3:30 this afternoon. Could you come then?"

I sank into a chair. I wanted to see a doctor right now, but I knew I would survive until afternoon. "Sure. Thanks. I'll be there at 3:30."

I called in sick at the print shop. I no more felt like peddling my bike than I felt like climbing Mount Rushmore, but since that was my only form of transportation, I knew that's what I'd have to do. So I climbed on my trusty old bike and headed for the doctor's office.

After I had filled out several forms, a nurse called my name and ushered me into one of the examination rooms. She instructed me to strip down to my undershorts, put on this ridiculous gown, and concluded by telling me the doctor would be in soon.

"Good afternoon, Charles," Dr. Jones greeted me a few minutes later. "What seems to be the problem?"

"For a start, I have a splitting headache, I'm having trouble breathing, and I ache all over."

"I see," he said thoughtfully as he pulled a little light from his pocket. "Open your mouth." He shone the light in my mouth while holding my tongue down with a little stick. As his probe touched one of my teeth, I groaned aloud. He touched another spot, and I had to hold onto the sides of the table to keep from writhing in pain.

Continuing his examination, he stuck his cold stethoscope on my chest and had me lie down while he poked and prodded my stomach. "Uh-huh," he mused again.

Finally he said, "Charles, you have terrible teeth. Several are badly infected. You must see a dentist immediately and get them pulled. The infection is spreading toxins through your whole body. That's why you feel so miserable."

He might as well have told me I had to fly to Argentina by nightfall. I had no money for dentists. I groaned and told him, "Thanks."

"Charles, I am serious," Dr. Jones persisted. "Unless you get those teeth removed, you will remain a very sick man and you won't live to see age 21."

I hated to do it, but I confessed that I had no money and there was no way I could even think about going to see a dentist. "And," I continued, "I don't know how I am going to even pay you. But thank you for your time," I ended lamely.

Slowly I redressed then exited past the receptionist. "I will pay the doctor when I can," I murmured as I slunk out the door.

Luckily, the trip home was slightly downhill or I don't think I could have made it on my bike. I parked it, dragged myself to my room, and fell on my bed. My head pounded, and my body ached from head to toe. I was too sick to fall asleep, but too sick to get up. I don't know how long I lay there, feeling totally miserable. I vaguely remember hearing a knock.

"Come in," I croaked. I looked up to see H. C. Hartman, the Union College business manager, enter my room. My heart nearly stopped beating! What was he doing here? Was he going to tell me I had to quit school because my bill was too high?

"Uh, yeah, hello Professor Hartman," I gulped. "Have a chair." I pointed to the only chair in my room.

"Hello Charles." Mr. Hartman took the chair I offered him.

"Uh, what are you doing here?"

"I've come to send you to a dentist," Mr. Hartman answered matter-of-factly. "Dr. Jones just called and told me what he told you—that unless you get all the infected teeth pulled, you won't live to see your next birthday."

"Look, Professor Hartman," I said, raising myself up on the bed. "I don't have any money. If he told me it would cost 40 dollars, he might as well say it would cost 4 million. I don't have the money."

"Well, I've made an appointment for you with Dr. LeRoy Gilbert for 10:00 tomorrow morning. We'll work out the money later. Just go." With that, Hartman stood, smiled at me, and left.

Dumbfounded, I sat dazed. "Hard Cash Hartman," students called him, yet here he was offering to "work out the money" later. What a miracle! To me, this kind man was never "Hard Cash Hartman" again! His caring attitude showed me what true Christianity is all about.

Dutifully, I showed up at Dr Gilbert's office the next day.

"I'm Charles Harris," I told the receptionist. "I'm here for my appointment."

"OK, good. You'll need to fill out some information for us, if you please," she said as she handed me a clipboard.

I filled out the forms and handed them back to the receptionist, then waited.

"Charles Harris," I heard someone call.

I'd never been in a dentist's office before, so I watched, fascinated, as someone clipped a bib around my neck, told me to swish some awful tasting stuff, then spit it in that "thing" with water swirling inside.

Dr. Gilbert had steel instruments that hurt much worse than Dr. Jones' had. He poked, picked, tapped, and probed. The pain caused me to groan and moan in spite of my resolve to be brave. I thought he would never stop poking in my mouth.

"Charles, what in the world have you done to create such bad teeth?" he asked me after he'd finished digging around in my mouth. I couldn't help it, but a rueful smile tugged at the right side of my mouth.

"Would eating only at Smith Brothers Ice Cream Shop explain anything? Like ice cream sundaes, milkshakes, ice cream bars, then throw in some of their chili beans for good measure, and add some hamburgers?"

"Did I understand you correctly?" Dr. Gilbert interrupted. "*Only* at the ice cream shop?"

"Yep, until two months ago," I replied. "After my mother threw me out of the house when I was 15, I worked there from 6:00 in the evening till 2:00 in the morning seven days a week. They let me eat as much as I wanted for free. I couldn't afford to buy food to eat in my room, so whatever I ate, I ate there, then nothing more till the next afternoon."

Dr. Gilbert knew about my mother, and he just nodded his head. Neither he nor most other people knew how I'd been surviving.

"Well, it's caught up with you, I'm afraid. Your teeth are a rotten mess. Seven of them are so badly infected that we'll have to pull them. Thankfully, penicillin is now available, and I think we can save the rest of them with a course of antibiotics."

"Look, Dr. Gilbert, I don't know how to say this, but I simply can't afford either the penicillin or to have my teeth pulled."

"Mr. Hartman has explained your situation," he assured me. "He and I have an agreement worked out that the college will pay for your treatment and add it to your college bill. He says you are an honest man and a good worker." I was shocked! "Hard Cash Hartman" was truly a miracle!

With the dental work behind me, I began to feel healthier and healthier. I'm sure it also helped that I was getting decent meals at the college cafeteria.

Speech class proved to be the most difficult. It challenged everything in me. My first speech was a total disaster. "I w-w-want to t-t-talk about Napoleon," I began. I'd chosen him from a list of topics we could speak about. "He was a g-g-g-great general though he was s-short."

While I'd always been a bit hesitant about speaking in public, during that speech, I couldn't stop stuttering. Worse, I dropped my cue cards, causing me to get information mixed up. *Disastrous,* I muttered to myself. The second speech wasn't quite as bad, but I was convinced in my heart of hearts that I would never be a preacher.

The heavy work schedule at the College Press combined with my job at the commercial print shop added up to nearly full-time work, leaving little time to study. As the semester drew to a close, I feared for my grades, and I panicked the day the grades were handed out. I eyed the envelope from the registrar's office like it was about to pounce on me, and I wondered whether I should open it or just toss it in the trash. Finally, I slipped my finger under the sealed edge and drew out the paper inside. I blinked, and blinked again: Freshman Composition—B; General Psychology—C; Introduction to Chemistry—B+; Life and Teachings of Jesus—A-; Speech—C; Medical Cadet Corps—A.

What a miracle! I must not be as stupid as Anna kept telling me I was.

The second semester seemed to go by more quickly, and my grades were almost as good. I threw myself into overtime work during the summer vacation to earn enough to pay off my first year's school debt and the dentist's bill. I applied everything I earned at the College Press to my college account. The commercial press paid more per hour, and in cash, so I lived off only that income.

I again registered for theology in the fall semester of my second year, but with secret thoughts of just quitting school altogether. Somewhere in the middle of that term, Dean Ogden called me into his office.

"Charles, I hear good reports from the College Press. They say you are developing into a skilled printer. I know you feel that God has called you to be a minister, but I urge you to seriously consider changing your major. I don't think you have what it takes to be a minister. Perhaps you should take up business and think about making printing your life's work. Frankly, Charles, I feel that you are wasting both your time and money, because I believe, Charles, that you'll never be a preacher."

His advice was not due to my grades, which were just above average, in spite of my heavy work schedule. But I had difficulty talking with people easily. A childhood of constant rejection and being told how stupid I was had severely damaged my self-image, causing me to withdraw, and making it difficult for me to make friends.

Disheartened, I left Dean Ogden's office. What should I do? I was trying to make myself good and felt that I was succeeding to a degree. Alone in my room, I fell to my knees. "My Father, what should I do?" I prayed aloud. "Am I really wasting my time? Do You want me to train to be a minister? Is Dean Ogden right? Should I just quit and go into full-time printing? What do *You* want me to do?" No answers flashed into my mind. No voice whispered or thundered a reply. Uncertain, I felt that if my dad were still living, he would encourage me to finish out the school year. He'd always said, "A sharpened ax works better than a dull one." So I plugged on, working, studying, working, studying. I had little time for anything else.

But Dean Ogden's talk had made a deep impression on me. As if to cement that impression forever, the religion department chairman called me into his office and kindly advised me that I just wasn't "preacher material."

Chapter 13

MARDELL

Still trying to "make myself good," I decided that continuing with the singing band was one thing I could "do." Yet, it was really quite boring! I probably would have stopped going to the nursing home to sing to what I considered a bunch of incoherent, half-asleep old folks, but I continued for two reasons. First, I was doing something to make myself good. Second, young ladies also came every week. Several of them caught my attention. However, I was too shy to approach them directly, so I asked my friend Marty to help. "Just ask them if they're dating anyone else," I instructed Marty.

About two weeks later, Marty reported to me. "Ingrid, the girl who plays the piano, and Mardell, who has dark brown hair and sings alto, are both available—that is, not dating. And they're both interested in you."

"Thanks, Marty. Which one do you recommend" I asked.

"Hey, man. I'm not a matchmaker!" he shot back, raising his palms and taking a step back. "You'll have to decide that for yourself!"

It took me a couple more weeks to work up the courage to ask Ingrid for a date. She accepted. "You'll have to clear it with the dean of women," she said, "and she will ask you who your chaperone is. I suggest Ruby Case."

I made the arrangements with the dean and Ruby. The big day finally came, and I showed up at the girl's dorm at the appointed time. But one of them—I never learned which one—was really slow. I had to wait for almost half an hour! Finally they came, and we left the dorm to walk to the college's lyceum program.

After the program, we walked slowly toward the girl's dorm, where we sat in the parlor to visit. All Ingrid could talk about was herself, her accomplishments and ambitions. She never asked me anything about myself, and she hardly even gave me a chance to talk. Out of the corner of my eye, I saw Ruby trying to stifle several yawns until Ingrid's droning became too much to bear, and she fell asleep!

Because I was so shy, Ingrid overwhelmed me! And then she started dating someone else. Marty analyzed the situation and told me, "She wants to make you jealous so you'll pursue her."

I wasn't interested in playing games, so I turned my thoughts to Mardell. I caught her glancing in my direction several times during singing bands, and if I looked her way, she'd flash a shy smile and look down. *She actually smiled at me!* I beamed inside.

I'm still not quite sure how it happened, but Mardell Potter and I began dating. And whenever I was with her, life seemed brighter. As unaccustomed as I was to the dating game, I felt perfectly comfortable with her. Although somewhat reserved, she asked questions to draw me out, shared about her life as an only child growing up on a farm in northeastern Nebraska, and chatted pleasantly. We asked Ruby to become our regular chaperone, and she never fell asleep again—Mardell's stories were much too interesting.

As I sat at a cafeteria table eating lunch on September 21, 1941, Mardell, Marty, and several other friends gathered around me. "Surprise, Charles! Happy birthday!" Mardell beamed. "Now, see if you can blow out all 21 candles." Her eyes danced with joy as she held out the cake she'd baked and decorated for me. The group burst out into "Happy birthday to you . . ." I could hardly keep the tears back. It was the first birthday party I'd ever had!

We were all poor college students, but each one of my friends thrust a card into my hands. "You can do it, Charles," Marty had scrawled in his card. "I have faith in you." My heart skipped a beat when Mardell handed me her card. I opened it expectantly and read what she'd written: "With God you can achieve any dream He gives you!"

As Christmas vacation approached, Mardell asked me if I would like to visit her home in northeastern Nebraska. Being quite "proper," I told her that I would need an invitation from her parents. A couple of weeks later, in mid-December, Mardell handed me a sealed envelope addressed to me that had been enclosed with one to her. I tore it open while she watched. The handwritten words from Mr. and Mrs. Potter immediately encircled me with warmth.

"Dear Charles," it said, "Mardell has been sharing with us about you, and we'd love to welcome you to our home for Christmas vacation. With war having just been declared, times ahead may be uncertain, but we are certain that we want you to come home for vacation." I looked at Mardell. Our eyes met, and I grinned. "Yes, I'll go home with you—since your parents have invited me."

I had never, ever, experienced a "family Christmas" before. Talk about nervous! How would I know how to act? My picture of "home" was stained with arguing, blaming, shaming, no peace, and no love toward me. I prayed some serious prayers! *Lord, I know I really like Mardell, and I feel comfortable in her presence, but I'm not sure about how her parents will feel toward me. My own future is so uncertain with this war. Just lead me, I pray.*

I bought a lovely light blue wool scarf for Mardell and had the store clerk wrap it for me. *This package must look pretty,* I told myself, *to make up for the very simple gift inside.*

I'd learned somewhere along the way how to carve soap, so I chose a big bar of Ivory soap to carve Mardell's dad a pair of praying hands. Mardell showed me how to make potholders from yarn and told me that her mom's favorite colors were pink, mauve, and white. I didn't have a clue what mauve was, so Mardell helped me pick out some yarn. With her help, I made a set of four potholders for her mother. *They really are quite pretty,* I thought to myself. *I hope she likes them.*

The 250-mile train ride from Lincoln to Mardell's hometown in Lynch, Nebraska, took several hours, and we visited the whole way. As the train rolled into the station, Mardell was so excited she couldn't stay seated. "There he is! There's my dad! The big tall man with the red cap and dark blue jacket!"

She jumped from the train into his arms, and they hugged and kissed. "Mom didn't come, because she's fixing a special dinner to welcome the two of you home," her dad explained. Turning to me, he didn't even wait for an introduction. "You must be Charles. Welcome to Lynch!" he boomed.

Suitcases loaded in the trunk, we headed for "home." It wasn't a long ride to their farm, and Mardell and her Dad chatted easily, including me in their conversation. From the moment I entered the house, I felt accepted. Their simple home exuded love.

"We're so glad you chose to spend this holiday with us!" Mardell's mother said. "I'm sorry we don't have a guest room, but you can put your things in the corner of the front room."

Formalities over, Mr. Potter invited me to join him in the barn for evening chores. "Just call me Harold," he said. The smell of hay, chicken feed, and farm animals assaulted my nose. I had never been so close to a live cow or chickens! Would you like to try your hand at milking Betsy?" Harold asked.

"Well, sir, I g-g-grew up in the city. I don't know anything about c-c-cows."

"I'll show you," he said simply. He pulled up a three-legged milking stool close to Betsy's back end and put both hands under her belly. "You hold two tits in your hands like this," he said, leaning back so I could see. Then you squeeze, starting up close to the udder—that's the big bag that holds all the milk—and gently pull while moving the squeezing motion away from the udder. As you squeeze and gently tug, the milk comes out, one squirt at a time. It's easier if you lean your head against her belly. First you milk the two tits closest to you, and then, when there's no more milk in them, you move to the two farthest from you."

Squirt, squirt, squirt. The milk hitting the pail made sort of a metallic sound.

"Meow," a cat purred as she rubbed against Harold's leg.

"Hey little girl. Open your mouth, Missy," he said as he directed a squirt of milk, not into the pail, but into the cat's open mouth. Then turning to me he said, "This is Missy, and when she hears me start to milk, she shows up for a nice warm treat." Missy swallowed the first squirt and opened her mouth for another.

"OK, Missy, that's enough for now. You'll get a bowl of it when we're finished," Harold promised as he continued to squirt milk into the pail. She seemed to know the routine, so she sat on her haunches, purring while she cleaned her face with her paws.

"It's good to have a cat in the barn," Harold said, reaching over and scratching behind Missy's ears. "Helps control the mouse population. Now, back to milking. Squeeze, gently pull, that's all there is to milking. Want to try?"

I'd declined once and felt I dare not decline again. As Harold rose from the stool, I wondered if I could do this. I sat down on the stool and started to move toward Betsy.

"Not quite so close to her back feet," Harold cautioned. "If she gets a notion to, she might kick either you or the bucket of milk."

OK, I thought to myself. *If I'm going to impress him, I've got to do this right!* I moved closer to Betsy's midsection, leaned my head against her belly, and marveled at its warmth and soft feel. Gingerly I grabbed the two tits closest to me and began squeezing from the top as I gently tugged and kept squeezing toward the end. Amazing! Milk squirted out! *I can do this! I can milk a cow!* I exulted to myself.

Harold encouraged me as he stood watching. "You're a quick learner, Charles. Good job! You keep milking while I feed the chickens. I'm right here in the barn with you, but you don't need me to stand and watch you."

He praised me! Said I was a quick learner! I felt like shouting out loud, to tell the whole world that I wasn't a failure, that I wasn't stupid!

My hands began to ache, unaccustomed to such work. But I would rather have died than not finish the job. Harold had to show me how to "strip" each of the four tits to get out the last bit of milk. Pounding me on the back, he said, "Great job, Charles! Thanks for the help!"

Harold carried the pail of milk to Missy's bowl and poured out a generous amount. Then we walked to the back porch, where he showed me a strange contraption with a handle that could turn round and round. He poured the pail of milk into the contraption, explaining, "This separates the cream from the milk. There's nothing to it—just crank that handle round and round, and be sure there are containers under each spout!" I watched in fascination as the cream went into a smaller container, and the milk into a larger one.

"We use most of the cream to make butter," Harold told me. "The sale of butter and extra eggs helps keep Mardell in college."

You mean her parents help her pay her school bill? I wondered. I had never even thought of the luxury of someone helping pay mine. I felt no twinge of jealousy, just joy for Mardell. Her parents loved her. What must that feel like?

After a sumptuous meal of baked potatoes and gravy, lentil soup, and lots of vegetables, I wasn't sure I could hold a piece of the blackberry pie that was cooling on the window sill. But, as with most college men, my legs were "hollow," so I managed to stow away the pie, too. *Never have I tasted such a wonderful meal,* I thought to myself. *And there wasn't a single argument! No shaming! Just wonderful companionship and exchanging of ideas. Amazing!*

Harold even joined in helping do the dishes, so I tried to make myself useful by sweeping the floor. Then I noticed the wood box was nearly empty. I'd seen the pile of wood on our way to the barn and I knew very well how to fill a woodbin with the pieces all laid in a row, not just dumped in. *Thank you, Anna,* I thought. *That's one good thing you taught me!*

A constant flow of good-natured banter got the job done in what seemed only minutes.

"OK, family, let's gather round the table for family worship," Harold announced. We all pulled up chairs to the table, and Harold led out in a simple but deeply spiritual time of praise and worship. Mardell's mom's prayer sounded like she was just talking to her best friend. She thanked God for Mardell's and my safe arrival and invited Jesus to watch over us as we slept.

"OK, gang," Harold announced, "it's getting late, and tomorrow's another day. Time for bed."

The effects of the long train ride, the strain of wanting to make a good first impression, milking the cow—all seemed to show up at once, and I rubbed my worn-out eyes. Neither I nor Mardell needed a second invitation. We wished each other a good night's sleep, and I headed toward the front room.

A medium-sized Christmas tree already stood in the corner, waiting for Mardell to help decorate. She explained that she loved to decorate the tree, so she had begged her parents to wait until she was home to put on the simple ornaments.

There were still two days until Christmas, so "Santa" hadn't arrived with any gifts yet. We popped popcorn and strung it on long pieces of thread, interspersed with dried red rose hips. We cut out paper snowflakes from folded paper and hung them on the tree. A string of lights had to be tested before they were added, because a single burned-out bulb would cause the whole string to remain unlit.

Mardell and her mom must have been very busy on Christmas Eve while Harold and I were in the barn, because when we returned, there were gifts under the tree, a pumpkin pie cooling on the windowsill, and the most wonderful smells of food inviting us to the table.

After everyone was in bed, I couldn't keep from peeking, and I slipped off the couch to carefully inspect each package. There were gifts for Mardell, Harold, and Mardell's mom, but I didn't find a single one for me. Even though I knew better than to expect one, still I felt that old familiar tug at my heart, while the old "tapes" started playing in my head. *You're stupid. You'll never amount to anything. You don't deserve any gifts.* I knelt beside the sofa and opened my heart to God. *I know I haven't known them for long, and I know I shouldn't expect any gifts, but Lord, You know how hungry I am for love! You know how I long to be part of a family. Please, Father, take away my disappointment. Let me just enjoy their joy.*

I don't know how long I prayed, but the empty, lonesome feeling was gradually replaced with the warm glow of Jesus' love and acceptance in my heart. I thought of an old song I'd heard, "No, never alone, no never alone. He promised never to leave me, never to leave me alone." Then, a verse I'd memorized long ago for a Bible class popped into my mind. "I have loved thee with an everlasting love" (Jeremiah 31:3). I felt the power of that promise. Yes, I could enjoy Christmas without gifts. Just being in a loving Christian home was enough. I slipped my gifts for them under the tree and lay down to sleep.

The next thing I knew, it was morning!

After the milking and other barn chores were done, we ate a "Christmas breakfast" of fresh-baked cinnamon rolls, scrambled eggs, cereal, and fruit. Harold announced, "Alright, everyone, let's get the table cleared quickly, and then we'll read the Christmas story. Mardell, would you open the doors to the front room so it can begin warming up while we do the dishes? I'll join you here in the kitchen to help as soon as I light a fire in the fireplace."

Breakfast chores finished, we all took a chair around the table and Harold read Matthew's and Luke's reports of the miraculous birth of Jesus. We talked a bit about the wonder of the incarnation and the even greater wonder that Jesus would risk leaving heaven to come show us what the Father was like.

"Ho, ho, ho," chanted Harold in his deepest voice after we gathered around the Christmas tree. "Look what Santa brought for Mardell. Here you are, sweetie."

It was my gift to her, and I watched as she wiggled her feet in anticipation, all the while carefully avoiding tearing the paper. "We use the paper year after year," she explained. She squealed with joy as she unfolded the scarf and wrapped it around her neck. "Thank you so much," she said, as she gave my hand a squeeze.

Apparently, "Santa" made a return visit while Harold and I were in the barn, because the next gift was one I hadn't seen. It was Mardell's gift to her mom.

Harold carefully scrutinized each package before delivering it. Some he set down, saying, "Not yet." When he picked up my gift to him, he grinned as he gently slid his finger under the paper. Seeming genuinely pleased as he pulled out the praying hands, he set the carving on the mantel, saying, "Now we will have prayers ascending continuously from our home."

I can honestly say I was at peace about not getting any gifts. After all, that's the way it had always been.

"Well, well, what do you know! Charles, it looks like you've been a good boy this year, so Santa has left you a gift." I felt reasonably sure it would be from Mardell, but when I looked at it, the tag said "From Mardell's Mom and Dad."

I felt a lump forming in my throat, and my eyes began to water. As the rest had done, I tried to open the package without tearing the paper with shaking hands and while trying not to cry. When I got the package open, there lay a beautiful, leather-bound, pocket-sized Bible with my name engraved on the cover. I was overwhelmed! As hard as I tried to hold them back, tears started running down my cheeks and I exclaimed, "Oh, thank you so much! It's beautiful. Thank you, thank you, thank you." I swiped my hand across my face and sniffled.

"Mardell has told us a little bit about your background," Mardell's mom volunteered. "We want you to know that you are a capable young man, and that you can become whatever God calls you to be. You'll be a success in life." She and Harold came over and sat down beside me and just wrapped me in their arms, holding me tightly in a bear hug. I buried my face in Harold's shoulder. My body shook as I wept. I don't know how long we sat there, but it must have been several minutes. Finally, I was able to regain my composure. "Thank you," I whispered. "You don't know how much this means to me!"

The gift-giving resumed. Harold handed me a package from Mardell's mom. Opening it, I drew out a pair of lovely black, gray, and yellow argyle socks. "Thank you," I said. She beamed. "I knitted them just for you. I hope they fit." And, of course, nothing would do but that I tried them on right then and there. They were a perfect fit! Emotions again overwhelmed me as I felt, for the first time in my life, a "mother's" love.

Next was a box of chocolate-covered cherries. "I think Mardell has been telling you what I especially like, too," I said as I grinned. "I absolutely love these candies!" And if that weren't enough, they gave me a bath towel and washcloth set and a big jar of mixed salted nuts. I couldn't believe it! Never had I had such a Christmas!

As soon as all the rest of the gifts had been opened and the papers carefully folded and stowed in the "Christmas wrapping" box, I excused myself and went for a long walk. "Lord," I prayed out loud, "You are so good to me. Thank You for a special Christmas and for this special family who have shown me such love and acceptance. If they can love this much in such a short time, how much greater is Your love for me!" I promised God that I would faithfully follow wherever He would lead.

The vacation ended too soon, and Mardell and I boarded the train back to Lincoln and Union College. The routine of classes, work, and study started once again. Soon, we would write the final exams for the semester—my third one in college.

Little did either of us sense how drastically our lives were about to change!

Chapter 14

WHO AM I?

December 7, 1941. The Japanese Imperial Forces viciously attacked Pearl Harbor, and now President F. D. Roosevelt had declared war, first on Japan, and several days later, on Germany. We were catapulted into World War II. Draft boards quickly organized throughout the United States, and all males between the ages of 21 and 45 were required to register.

In February 1942 I opened my mailbox and saw a government letter. Sensing it had information I didn't want to receive, I tore the envelope open slowly and pulled out the dreaded form.

"Greetings. You must appear for a medical examination to determine your fitness to serve your country if called. Bring your birth certificate and appear on February 28 at 10:00 a.m."

On the appointed day, I met a kindly doctor who performed a rather perfunctory exam. "You are physically fit to enter the army," he announced.

I had passed my physical, but at the next desk I discovered I had a problem—a big problem. "Please show me your birth certificate," the clerk at the processing desk instructed stoically.

"I don't have one," I replied.

"Why didn't you bring it with you, per the letter's instructions?" she queried, her tone of voice unchanged.

"I don't have one to bring and have no earthly idea how or where to get one," I answered.

Finally making eye contact with me, she curtly informed me that getting a birth certificate was my problem, not hers. "And," she brusquely added, "you have exactly two weeks to find it and report back. Dismissed!"

My walk with God was becoming more personal and real, and I prayed through the rest of that day and the following one that God would show me what to do.

In my work at the commercial print shop, I was given the task of setting the type, preparatory to printing some letterheads and envelopes for a

Curtis Swain, Attorney at Law. As I was setting the type, I sensed God impressing me that Curtis Swain could help me, although I had never met him and knew nothing about him. I told my boss about my problem and asked if he thought the man could help me.

"Well, Charles, you *are* in a pickle." He furrowed his eyebrows and stroked his chin. "But you know what? I am sure Mr. Swain would be happy to help you."

On the second day after my visit to the recruiting office, Mr. Swain came to pick up his order. I saw my boss take him into his office, and a few minutes later they both approached me. The racket of machines made conversation all but impossible without shouting, so I shut off my machine and my boss introduced us.

"This is Charles, and he's got a bit of a problem," my boss said. The boss motioned us to his office where we both sat down.

"Tell me about your problem, Charles," Mr. Swain invited.

"My parents told me I was born September 21, 1920, in Colorado Springs," I explained. "My dad died when I was 15 years old, and my mother kicked me out of the house a couple of weeks later. I've seen my mother three times since then, once across several aisles at a grocery store, and twice at church, but haven't spoken with her. Kids at school used to tease me about being adopted, but when I tried to talk with Mother, she told me it was a lie and to never talk about it again. When I asked my dad about it, he said he'd talk with me about it 'sometime later'—but then he died. So I don't know if I'm adopted or not," I explained.

"What's your mother's name? Is she still living at the same address? Do you know if she's home during the day?" He asked several other questions.

After giving him all the information I knew, I said, "The draft clerk gave me just two weeks to find my birth certificate and report back on March 14."

Our heads turned toward the nearby wall calendar. "Whew," Mr. Swain whistled. "Just 12 days left. I'll do what I can." He slapped me on the back and said, "Don't worry, young man."

"Thank you, sir. I appreciate it," I said, feeling a burden already rolling off my shoulders.

God, thank you for sending Mr. Swain, I prayed as I walked back to my machine. *I trust You and him to solve my problem. He told me not to worry, so I'm trusting.* I kept on praying. I had no idea what would happen to me if I couldn't produce a birth certificate, but I could imagine dire consequences.

Just five days before the deadline, Mr. Swain returned, and my boss called me into his office, then left me alone with Mr. Swain.

"Well, Charles, we have a bit of a problem here," he began.

"Uh, couldn't you find my birth certificate?" I asked anxiously.

"Don't worry about that, Charles. I have it right here in my briefcase," he said, tapping the leather case. "The problem is that you aren't who you think you are."

"Excuse me?" I said, perplexed.

"The name Harris that you've used all your life isn't your legal name."

"What? I don't understand." Suddenly, Susie's ceaseless chant, "You're adopted," began playing once again in my head.

Mr. Swain continued, "Your birth father gave you up for a 'no contact' adoption. That means that, legally, he could never contact you again—ever. He signed the legal document. I have it in my briefcase, as well. Lewis and Anna Harris picked you up from your father along with the adoption papers. They took you to their home, but . . . ," and here he paused. "They never filed the papers your birth father signed to legalize your adoption!"

I was stunned! So I *was* adopted, yet Anna was also right when she said that I *wasn't*. My mind was racing a thousand miles an hour, yet it seemed to be moving in slow motion all at the same time. Susie's taunting mixed in my emotions with the bitterness I felt toward Anna, creating a sense of being deceived, betrayed. Had Mr. Swain not been there, I'd have stomped and screamed and yelled to get all the anger out of my system.

Pulling my thoughts back to the conversation, I squeaked, "So who am I?"

"That's up to you," he replied. "You have two options. Your first option is for me to go back to Anna Harris and see if I can convince her to complete the adoption that she and her husband never finished. You are not legally adopted to that family and never have been." He paused for a moment to let the importance of that statement sink in, then continued.

"The other option is for you to take the last name of your birth father. Since you applied for your Social Security number using the name "Harris," I'll have to file some papers for you to get that information changed. Any other official papers, such as school credits and the like, will also need to be changed. I'll be glad to help you with that as well, if you choose to go that route."

Slowly the full meaning of what Mr. Swain had told me began to sink in. I was not Charles *Harris!* Suddenly, I felt like jumping up and dancing and shouting! I could actually get rid of that hated name "Harris!" I cared about my "father," Lewis Harris, but a thrill pulsed through me as I realized that I actually had valid reason to put Anna forever out of my life!

And then the question came back to me. *Who am I—really? What is my real name?* My mind was in turmoil. I had never thought about the possibility of changing my name—especially not at age 21! But Dad Harris was dead, and the thought of going back to Anna was out of the question! Finally, I said, "I have no desire to have any more dealings with her or to carry the Harris name if it isn't mine."

"Well, that settles it," Mr. Swain announced. "I think you have made a wise choice. Anna Harris was one tough woman to deal with. I had a hard time getting this document from her, and even if you wanted to, I'm not sure she would go ahead with the adoption." With that, he reached into his briefcase and handed me my birth certificate. For the first time in my entire life, I read my father's name and discovered who I *really* was: Charles L. White, Jr.

In the next five days Mr. Swain miraculously managed to fill out the necessary forms to change my name on all my official government records and submit a letter of explanation to the draft board. The Lord had worked a great miracle for me, and now, for the first time in my life, I knew who I really was—Charles L. White. *I like White much better than Harris,* I thought.

In Medical Cadet training, a required course for all male Union College freshmen, we'd been taught to request a 1-A-O classification if drafted. This would allow us to serve as medics, still in the line of fire, but not expected to bear arms and take human life. Consequently, at the time of my registration with the draft board, I made that request, and it was granted. Soon I received an official card from the government, which I was to present if I was inducted.

This would play a vital part in the next miracle God would work on my behalf!

Chapter 15

FAMILY

How can I know if I'm in love and not just infatuated? What's the difference between true love and puppy love? I wondered. Not having any close male friends, and without a mom or dad, how was I supposed to figure out the answer to such weighty questions? One thing I knew for sure. Ever since the school year ended and Mardell returned to her home for the summer, I was lonesome! I missed her more than I ever thought I could miss a human being. I kept thinking of things I wanted to share with her—then realize glumly that she was not there.

Of course, there was the mail. I wrote to her faithfully, and she responded immediately. But to have to wait a week for delivery of the letters bearing her comments on some idea, her opinion on some question, or just her thoughts about life in general—just seemed intolerable!

However, love will always find a way, and even though it seemed terribly expensive to a poor printer, I found the money for a train ticket to Lynch, Nebraska, and arranged with my boss for some vacation time in July 1942.

As the train marked off the distance mile by mile, it seemed as if it was moving at a turtle's pace. Would we never reach Lynch? Of course, I knew before I started the journey that it would take hours. The same trip with Mardell for Christmas vacation had streaked by like a flash of lightning over the Nebraska plains, but in this one, the train seemed to be tiptoeing as if trying not to disturb them.

Should I remain in my seat by the window, or should I be at the door, ready to jump down? I should probably wait in my seat, so I could see where Mardell is standing. No, there won't be that many people on the platform, so I can easily spot her. I argued back and forth with myself until I nearly drove myself crazy!

Finally, there was only one more train stop, which meant my station was only about half an hour away. I simply couldn't sit still, so I lifted my suitcase from the overhead rack and walked to the door. I could feel the train slowing, and it finally lumbered to a stop. It didn't take me even two seconds to alight from the train the moment the door opened. And there she was! We flew into each other's arms and kissed, while Harold waited discretely some distance away.

We walked hand in hand toward Harold, who greeted me with a big bear hug. "Glad to see you again, young man," he beamed as he pounded me on the back. Back at the house, Mardell's mom greeted me just as warmly with a less bear-huggy, but just as warm, embrace. Once again, I felt more like one of the family than a visitor. I felt like I had come home.

Hidden in the depths of my travel bag was a small watch in a velvet-covered case. I wasn't sure just when or how I would present it to Mardell, along with the most important question any man can ever ask the woman of his dreams.

On the second day of my visit, Mardell and I borrowed the family car and drove toward the Missouri river, about a mile north of their farm. On the way, at the end of their long driveway, we stopped to pick up the mail.

"Electric bill, gas bill, something from Aunt Mary and Uncle Don," Mardell said. "And what's this? It's addressed to you. Someone—probably your roommate—forwarded it here," she said as she slid back into the front seat, handing me the envelope. I took it and noticed it was from California, from someone I didn't know. I tossed the letter on the seat. I had more important things on my mind than a mysterious letter from a stranger.

Approaching a giant elm tree near the river, I parked the car, and we got out. A grassy spot under the tree offered relief from the shimmering heat of the Nebraska noonday summer sun. Fields of golden yellow ripened grain waved around us, signaling the imminent harvest. As Mardell and I settled on the blanket under the elm leaves rustled by a gentle breeze, we could see and hear the Missouri River just a stone's throw away. I'd slipped the watch case into my pocket when she wasn't looking.

We sat hand in hand, and I marveled at her beauty. She'd tied her long, dark curls back with a light blue ribbon that matched the dress she was wearing. I knew the answer to my questions about love.

My heart pounded in my chest, and I wondered if she could hear it. Knowing exactly what I wanted to say, my tongue refused to cooperate, seeming to be tied in knots. The tree, the river, the golden grain, all seemed a million miles away as our eyes locked. It was right. My heart stopped pounding and the words escaped my lips as softly as the gentle breeze around us: "I love you."

She held my gaze while her delicate lips joined her dancing eyes in the sweetest smile I'd ever seen.

"Mardell," I said, "will you marry me?"

71

She leaned her head into my chest and trembled as my arms encircled her. I felt a warm trickle run down my arm. Somehow, I knew the answer even though she hadn't said it. We just sat there holding each other. Finally, she lifted her head, looked into my face and whispered, "Yes!" We sealed our promise to love each other forever with a long embrace and kiss.

Digging the watch case out of my pocket, I showed it to her. She squealed delightfully as she lifted the watch from its velvet protection and put it on her right wrist. We sat a bit longer, just absorbing the beauty of the grain fields, the river, and the love flowing between our hearts.

What a contrast with the news reports of the war raging in Europe and the Pacific! Mardell and I both realized that, as a young male, I could be inducted into the army at any time. So as we dreamed of a blissful wedded future, we also knew that now was not the time to start making plans.

Returning to the car, I spotted the mysterious letter. Opening it, I read aloud. "Dear Charles. You don't know me, but I'm your Aunt Lottie. My sister Lois and I cared for you after your mother died. Your father fought against putting you up for adoption, but in the end, there seemed no other way."

I glanced at Mardell as if to give myself time for the words to sink in. She put her hand on my shoulder as I turned back to the letter.

"According to the adoption papers your father signed, he was never to have any contact with you. But when we learned that you had taken your real name back, we figured something about your adoption had changed and that the 'no contact' order was no longer in force. That's why I've written this letter. Your birth dad is still alive . . ."

Mardell's eyes searched my face, trying to gauge my reaction. I continued reading.

". . .and I am writing for him to see if you would be interested in making contact with your real family. You have four brothers and one sister still living, plus aunts, uncles, and cousins. I know this letter must come as a shock to you. There is so much history that you do not know, but I hope you'll consider writing to your birth father through me and consider meeting us. Sincerely, your Aunt Lottie."

I had never even faintly considered trying to locate my birth family, and this letter didn't change anything. Although I was curious why my birth father put me up for adoption, this question, my birth father and family, this letter—all of it—just didn't fit into the picture Mardell and I had just painted of our commitment to each other. She had accepted my proposal! For the first time in my experience, life was finally beginning to look good to me. I felt no need or desire to complicate my life by trying to get acquainted with people I didn't know.

I read the letter to Mardell again. "What are you going to do?" she asked gently.

"Nothing."

"You mean you don't want to find out about your real father?"

"No," I answered blankly. "He gave me away, so he must not have loved me."

"You really don't know, Charles. There's probably a long story behind it that you'll never know if you don't contact him."

We drove back to the house in near silence, each of us deep in thought.

"Can I tell my mom and dad about the letter?" Mardell asked quietly.

"Oh sure," I replied. "What difference does it make? I've never met them, and you and your mom and dad are my family now."

She smiled and squeezed my hand. "You *are* part of our family, even though we won't be married until this crazy war ends," she said softly. "My mom and dad have loved you ever since they first met you."

"You know, I could feel their love and acceptance. So why should I make contact with a stranger who just happens to be my birth father?"

"Well, let's not think about it right now," Mardell replied. "But, can we just read the letter to mom and dad?"

I agreed.

Mardell couldn't wait for me to finish parking the car. As soon as I stopped, ready to back into its spot, she jumped from the car and flew into the house.

"Mom, Dad, come look!" she squealed, as she held out her arm for them to see the watch. "Oh Mom, he asked me to marry him!"

By then I'd joined her, and Harold grinned, "Well, it's about time, man! What took you so long? We thought you'd never pop the question!"

Mardell's mom laughingly scolded, "Now, Harold, you be nice to him!"

"He knows me well enough to know I'm just kidding. Welcome to the family, Charles. If you want, you can now call us Mom and Dad.

"Mom!" At last I'd found "my" mom!

Again, feelings of amazement and love washed over me. As the four of us all hugged each other, I knew that my heart had finally found a home, a mom, and a dad. As at Christmas time, I couldn't help wiping a few tears from my eyes. As I gazed at Mardell, she was more beautiful than ever, and

I whispered in a choked voice, "I'll take care of her as long as I live!" Again, we all hugged and cried tears of joy together.

After supper, as we sat around the table, Mardell asked me in a whisper, "Can I share with them about the letter now?"

I agreed, even though I felt no need to meet my birth family when I had already found a family of my own. Handing it to Mardell, I asked her to read it.

As she finished reading, everyone's eyes were on me.

"Your mother died?" Mardell's mom gasped. "That's so sad!"

"You still have living brothers and sisters!" Harold exclaimed. "So, when are you going to write to your father? I can't imagine his pain at having to give you up for adoption. Neither can I imagine his excitement at learning where you are and that you are really still alive. I'd be dying to get to know more about you!"

Several times over the next day or so, one or another of them brought up the letter. "Don't you wonder what happened that would cause your father to give you up?"

"Charles, you might consider contacting them just to sort out your family history," Harold reasoned. All three of them gently urged me to at least write my Aunt Lottie and find out more about my lost family.

The vacation ended all too soon. The trip back to Union College seemed much shorter than the trip out, even though Mardell was not with me. As soon as I arrived in the dorm, I picked up my mail—two whole week's worth. I stuffed the envelopes under my arm and returned to my room to sort through them. There were letters from the college and a paycheck from the commercial printer. Then, I saw it. An envelope from the United States Army. My hands trembled as I tore it open.

"Greetings! You are to report for military duty at . . ."

My mind whirled. I was expecting the "invitation" from Uncle Sam, but the reality of it hadn't really hit me until now.

The shock of receiving my orders to report for military duty kept my mind so busy that it was a day or two before I remembered the letter from Aunt Lottie. Keeping my promise to Mardell and her parents, I wrote a brief letter to my aunt. In just a few days, I received my first letter ever from my own flesh and blood—my real father.

"Dear Charles," I read. "How often I have longed to find you. You will never know how hard it was for me to give you up for adoption after your mother died. I would love to get to know the son I loved so fiercely but had to give up because of circumstances. Please forgive me for abandoning you. I believed I had chosen a solid, loving Christian home where you could develop a fine Christian character and develop some roots. I would love to hear from you."

Yes, I do want to write to you, I thought. *But not too fast!*

We began exchanging infrequent letters, and eventually even photos of ourselves. He told me that he had remarried many years after my mother died, and that the entire family had moved to California. Slowly, we began to build a bond of respect and love.

Had I not been required to produce a birth certificate, and had the lawyer not obtained it for me, which alerted my birth family to who and where I was, I would never have found them. What a miracle!

But the miracles were only beginning.

Chapter 16

YOU'RE IN THE ARMY NOW!

Induction into the army at Fort Leavenworth, Kansas, presented a whole new world to me. Gruff, no-nonsense officers instructed us recruits to pack all our civilian clothes to be shipped home. We were to wear only government-issued clothing from now on. I especially hated to pack the argyle socks that Mardell's mom had knitted for me. They were a symbol of the family who had accepted me and loved me.

My uniform felt clumsy on my body. The government seemed to have two sizes—too big and too small, and I felt like I'd gotten both! I was supposed to salute almost everyone except other recruits like myself. I followed the rest of the newbies to a huge, open field. There, we were told to march to a Quonset hut lined with long tables. At one table we picked up our mess kit, which contained a bowl-like plate, spoon, fork, and knife, and a mug—all made of metal. At another table, we picked up our first aid kits.

It was the rifle table I dreaded. Man after man was called forward and handed his weapon. Then each one read the number on the butt of his rifle and signed for it. I cringed when the scowling sergeant barked "Next!" and I had to step forward. I *could* not, *would* not kill—even the enemy. I had promised God that I would remain true to what I believed from His Word, and I was prepared to stand my ground. Our medical cadet corps (MCC) instructor had told us we'd probably encounter pressure to accept our rifles, and he advised us to avoid the slick talk and refuse to take it. If we did take the weapon, he said, it would be much more difficult to refuse using it later. He also told us to have our 1-A-O registration card available immediately when we were challenged. I approached the desk.

"Name?"

"White."

"Take a rifle," the sergeant commanded, "and read me the number printed on the butt."

"Sir," I said, "I am a c-c-conscientious objector to k-k-killing. I was g-granted 1-A-O status by the d-d-draft board, so I won't n-need a rifle."

"You're a *what?*" the sergeant yelled.

"Sir, I'm a Christian who doesn't b-b-believe in killing. I c-c-can't t-take the rifle." I stuttered. *I sure wish I had my foster dad's speaking ability!* I thought. For an instant I forgot I was standing in front of this army sergeant, and I was back in my teen years. My world had started to collapse when my foster dad died, and it had totally collapsed when I had found my clothes boxed up on the porch with a note telling me, "I have taken care of you for the past 12 years and am no longer able to do it. Take your clothes and do not return. You are no longer welcome here."

The sergeant's stubby finger punching the air in front of me brought me back to the present.

"White, sign for it right here, take your rifle, and move to the next table!" he shouted.

"Sir," I persisted, and a surge of courage chased my stuttering away. "I am a Seventh-day Adventist and do not believe in killing. I have a 1-A-O card from army headquarters."

All he heard was resistance from this skinny kid in front of him. "You're in the army now, soldier!" the sergeant yelled, the tone of his voice a few notches higher. "Didn't anyone tell you there's a war going on? Now sign for this rifle, take it, and get out of here, you #*@#*!"

By now, everyone in the tent was staring at me.

I didn't budge. "Sir, here is my official government 1-A-O card issued by army headquarters in Washington, D.C." I held out my card.

"Yes, I see that fancy little card you are holding. I've never heard of such nonsense as this. Now you just be a good boy, sign for this rifle, and we will see about the matter later."

This was the moment my MCC instructor had warned about. I had a choice. I could take the rifle or stand my ground. For a long moment, the sergeant's beady brown eyes challenged mine. His eyes narrowed to slits, and a crimson color engulfed his face. Pulling himself to his full height, he inhaled deeply, and I prepared for a hurricane. With all the force that his 300-pound frame could support, he screamed, "White! Take this rifle and go!"

"Sir, I cannot take the rifle," I replied. I stilled the twitching of my fingers. "Sir, I am happy to serve my country, and I am not asking for safety from danger. The most logical place to serve would be in the medical corps," I said quietly.

My refusal finally began to sink in. He glared at me for a full 30 seconds. Then he jerked the rifle I was supposed to take and tossed it to one side. "We'll see about this," he spat out. "Be back here tomorrow morning at 0800 hours [8:00 a.m.]. You can tell your little tale to the captain in the morning." He dismissed me with a contemptuous fling of his hand. Spitting on the ground, and just missing my foot, he turned his back on me and called, "Next!"

The next morning, I made sure my uniform was spotless, my shoes were shined, and my hair was combed carefully. I saluted the captain as I approached his desk. My first impression was that he was much kinder than the sergeant. He gave me his full attention but was puzzled.

"What's this 1-A-O provision?" he queried. While his assistant checked with higher authorities, he asked me about my church, what I believed, and how I was able to get this special qualification. I answered his questions honestly, praying for wisdom to say just the right words. I assured him that 1-A-O status had not been created for just my church, that it was granted to any man who held conscientious objections to the taking of life.

Fifteen minutes later, the assistant returned and informed the captain that indeed I did have 1-A-O status and explained what it meant. The captain looked up at me and smiled. "Well, White, it looks like you've won your case!" he said.

I breathed a sigh of relief.

"So this means we have to give you a different assignment," the captain said. "Go back to your barracks, and I'll have someone bring you your new orders."

I returned to my barracks and didn't have long to wait. By mid-morning I was sent by jeep to the main post office on the base. A soldier escorted me inside and introduced me to another sergeant.

For the next two weeks I sorted mail all day long while the recruits who arrived on base the same time as I continued their basic training. I was learning nothing about military rules, but was thankful that I had completed the Medical Cadet Course, which had thoroughly trained me in the basics of military protocol.

Near the end of my second week sorting mail, my supervisor told me to report to the main medical building the following morning. Assuming that my request to be assigned to the Medical Corps was being granted, I arrived as ordered the next morning, only to learn that no transfer had come through yet. Instead, I was being assigned temporary duty giving immunization shots to the hundreds of men arriving daily at the huge army base.

I had never given a shot of any kind, nor had I even held a syringe in my hands before. I really pitied the first several dozen men as they endured my shaking hands and my efforts at being a medic!

When the 10-week basic training ended, everyone was reassigned to various stations throughout the United States. Although I had received no basic training, I received sealed orders to report to a specific office in Fort Knox, Kentucky, at the designated date and time. I was the only one out of hundreds to receive this order. Along with the order came the train ticket to take me to Louisville, Kentucky. It was rather exciting to ride in a Pullman car and eat three meals a day in the diner—all at government expense! When I arrived in Louisville, I was met by a serviceman who drove me to Fort Knox, about 35 miles from the train station.

The orders I carried with me were officially sealed, and I was instructed to give them only and directly to the officer specified by name on the outside of the envelope. I didn't have any idea where I was going or what would happen to me!

We pulled up in front of a large, three-story building covering almost a full block. Inside, I met the officer whose name was on the envelope, and handed it to him. He opened it, studied it for two or three minutes, then turned to me.

"White," he said, "because of your background in printing, you've been assigned as a pressman to work on one of the large presses in the official military's printing facility."

Not what I expected, I thought. I'd assumed I would be transferred to the Medical Corp, but here I was, assigned to work on a printing press. *Well God,* I prayed, *what miracle do You have awaiting me next?*

I entered the military printing building with trepidation, yet confident that God was watching over me. I'd passed the first test when I refused to take a gun. But one other test still lay ahead: the Sabbath. Believing strongly that God's Word forbade working from sundown on Friday to sundown on Saturday, I felt that I should take my stand immediately rather than waiting until the end of the day on my first Friday at work. So with a prayer, I took a deep breath and addressed the officer.

"Sir, I am a Seventh-day Adventist, and I have a 1-A-O classification. Seventh-day Adventists observe the seventh day of the week as the Sabbath, from Friday at sundown to Saturday at sundown. I am willing to work any hours, night or day, but I request Friday evenings and Saturdays off."

The officer's response was not what I expected. He actually smiled! "I know all about Seventh-day Adventists," he said. "You will have no problem working here. Normally, the entire shop is closed on Saturdays anyway."

What a miracle! My eight years working as a pressman were paying off in ways I would never have expected!

The officer motioned to me with his hand. "Follow me. I'll introduce you to the master sergeant who will be your immediate boss. He's in charge of the pressroom where you will work."

When I first saw my immediate supervisor, the first thing I noticed was his gestapo-type mustache. His bushy eyebrows came close to meeting in the middle as he scowled at me. A jagged scar ran down his left cheek. I immediately sensed that he didn't like me.

When I reported to work the next morning, I learned that I would be printing maps and other official items for the Army Corps of Engineers. I wondered what business I had as part of the Army Corps of Engineers but didn't ask questions.

The press I was to operate was exactly like the one at the print shop in Lincoln! I breathed a prayer of thanks for that and worked for about a month with no problems. The commanding officer sauntered by a time or two and complimented me on my work. However, I continued to feel that the master sergeant didn't like me. He never said anything negative, but his attitude was cold and distant. Nearly every Friday afternoon, he would bring me some big job, telling me it had to be done immediately. I hadn't spent the last eight years taking presses apart, oiling them, and working them for nothing, and every Friday, I would manage to complete the assignment before sundown.

Toward the end of the fifth week, the master sergeant came to me late Friday afternoon and told me he had a rush job that just *had* to be done the next day. When he showed me the job, I knew it was not an emergency. It was a job I'd seen in an area where we put "nonrush" jobs that could be done whenever we had time. I also knew that, in spite of my best efforts, I simply could not complete this job by sundown.

"Sir," I began, "my agreement with the commanding officer was that I would come in Saturday night or Sunday, but I need Friday night and Saturday off. I will be happy to finish this job Saturday night or Sunday."

The sergeant glared at me. "White, you *will* be here at 0800 in the morning, and you *will* finish that that job." The color in his face deepened from pink to crimson—all except for the jagged scar, which remained white. "That's an order!" he commanded as he turned and left the pressroom.

This was my first real Sabbath test. What should I do now? I could not go to the commanding officer without permission from the master sergeant. Army regulations forbade going over the head of one's supervising officer without permission, and I was sure the master sergeant would never grant me permission to see the company commander. Besides, he had probably already left for the weekend.

When I entered the army, I had made a serious commitment to God that I would stand firm for what I believed to be right, no matter the consequences. I spent the rest of Friday and well into the night in earnest petition to God for guidance and wisdom. I finally slept fitfully, but when I awoke the next morning, I felt rested and my mind was clear. I knew exactly what I should do.

I dressed in my Class A dress uniform and strode into the pressroom with my Bible under my arm a few minutes before 0800 hours, as I had been ordered. Promptly at 0800, the master sergeant walked into the room. When he saw me, he stopped abruptly and said, "What are you doing here in that uniform? I gave you an official order, and I expect it to be followed. Now get to work!"

"Excuse me, sir . . ." I began." But he interrupted me.

"White, you have deliberately disobeyed the direct command of a noncommissioned army officer, and I will see that you are punished to the full extent of the law for a serious offense in time of war." Again he scowled and his face reddened. His angry threat was beginning to really frighten me. "Now report to the commanding officer's desk immediately."

That, in fact, was what I'd wanted all along!

I sat in the commander's outer office until 1400 hours [2:00 p.m.]. He passed through the small outer office on his way to and from his inner office several times, but he gave no indication that I was there. I knew enough about military rules to not speak to him until he spoke to me. Finally, a couple of minutes after 1400 hours, he opened his door and called me into his office. I stood at attention in front of his desk while he gave me a stern lecture concerning military rules and my "crime" in disobeying orders, especially in time of war. He gave no permission for me to say a word. Could this be the same man who had told me there would be no Sabbath problems? It was he who had come back to my press and complimented me on at least two occasions. Now he seemed like a different man!

"White, this is the weekend. But I am placing you under arrest-of-quarters immediately. You will be escorted to your quarters and to and from chow at mealtime. You are not to leave your quarters for any reason or go anywhere without an M.P. [military police] escort. Monday morning you will be escorted back to my office, where I will sign the official papers for your court-martial. You will then be taken to the camp stockade to await your trial. Dismissed!"

I had not been allowed to say a single word.

As I exited his office, two M.P. officers stepped forward to escort me to my barracks. *Court-martial! Crime for disobeying orders!* Shaken to my core, I wondered if the officers could feel my body trembling as they led me by my arms.

The M.P.s left me at the door of my barracks. The place was empty. Most of the men had doubtless gone into Louisville for the weekend. I fell to my knees by my bunk and tears mingled with heartfelt prayers. Utterly exhausted from the mental stress, I crawled on top of the covers and fell into a deep sleep.

I don't know how long I slept, but it seemed only a moment when I awoke with a start. Two soldiers were standing by my bunk calling my name. My immediate thought was that they were military police coming to take me to the camp stockade. In my groggy state I failed to notice that they did not have the usual M.P. insignias.

"We are here with orders to move you immediately," they stated. I was taken aback by their friendliness. They helped me pack my clothes and carry them down to the jeep. My curiosity deepened as we pulled away from the barracks.

"I'm not supposed to ask you this," one of the soldiers shouted over the roar of the open vehicle, "but I was just wondering who you know to get an 'Urgent—For Immediate Action' assignment?"

I thought he was joking! When no laughter ensued, I realized he was serious. "What do you mean? Where are we headed?" I asked rather timidly.

Just about then we pulled up in front of a barracks with a sign in front that read, "Demonstration Regiment."

As we began to unload the Jeep, a sergeant and a corporal came out with a friendly, hearty welcome.

"Come in, White. We've been looking for you for more than two weeks." With that, they picked up my duffel bag and a smaller bag. "Follow us," they said. They led me to the barracks next door and to a private room on the second floor! They left my bags by the bed, and said, "Come over to the office after you are settled. We'll fix you up with a weekend pass. We can get acquainted on Monday. Our colonel sent through a request for your transfer to this company some time ago. Just this morning, we learned that your transfer had been held up in some office on the base. It's really hard to get things done on the weekend, but our commanding officer had the feeling that it was important to get you here this very day."

The sergeant then made out a pass and ordered a regiment driver to take me to the base bus station so I could catch a bus to Louisville. He told me how to get from the bus station to the USO, where servicemen can stay overnight.

My head was swimming from the rapidity of the whole thing. *White, do you believe in miracles?* I exclaimed to myself. The very day of my deepest need, God had worked on the hearts of a number of people to work together to get me a transfer to the Medical Corps, thus preventing a court-martial. Even better, the Demonstration Regiment was one of the most unique and prestigious regiments in the entire army!

For the next three years, until my discharge, I never had another problem with the observance of God's Bible Sabbath. I had proved faithful over the rifle incident, and now God had honored my stand for the Sabbath. He seemed content with my commitment to Him.

But God had still more outstanding miracles in store for me.

Chapter 17

IN THE MEDICS

The Demonstration Regiment existed to provide a final training for units slated for overseas duty. Set in the hills not far from Washington, D.C., this special "demonstration" consisted of an entire battle-ready battalion set up to resemble a typical battlefield. Here we staged mock battles of the various types the troops might face in either Europe or the Pacific. Every three weeks, new battalions and other guests arrived from throughout the Unites States and even foreign countries to watch as the Demonstration Regiment staged mock battles. The Medical Unit, to which I was assigned, served the medical needs of the entire regiment, in addition to the many visiting units.

I helped staff the dispensary on the base, where daily "sick call" was held. Other days, I served on field duty to assist in any emergency that might arise during the training sessions. Our medical unit consisted of four medical doctors, one executive officer who was not a doctor, and 20 enlisted men. We formed a rather close-knit team, and the friendliness and camaraderie between the men—even the officer—continually amazed me. We had nearly every weekend free, except for the occasional "charge-of-quarters," when we stayed at the dispensary from Friday through the next Monday morning to care for any emergency that might arise. I could not have hoped for a better assignment in the army!

After four months of work at Fort Knox I was sent to Fort Benjamin Harrison near Indianapolis, Indiana, for special training as a surgical technician. After completing that course I moved to the University of Ohio in Columbus, Ohio, for 10 more weeks of training. When I completed that training, I returned to Fort Knox, where I received a promotion, earning the title of Army Male Nurse skilled for surgical procedures.

Shortly after my return to Fort Knox, four men from our unit were given the task of creating a combat-type curriculum. It had to represent a combat unit as nearly as possible. We wrote a curriculum that consisted of five days of two-hour sessions per day, for a total of 10 hours. The visiting battalions were divided into groups of 100 to 125 to be taught how to stop bleeding, splint broken limbs, bandage severe wounds using whatever was available, and properly use a gas mask. After the curriculum received approval the other three men and I began teaching what we had written, adding how to maintain field sanitation and how to self-medicate with morphine upon receiving a serious injury with no available medical help. We processed four groups of 400 to 500 men every two hours.

Each day, I gave four two-hour lectures and demonstrations. With no public address system, my voice quickly grew strong, and I was able to speak easily, clearly, and confidently, even developing the ability to think on my feet. Here I was—the one who had been told that I would never make a preacher because of my hesitant speech—teaching hundreds of men every day!

Letters between Mardell and me kept the mail service busy. She wrote longer letters than I, but I answered every one. I described my work, and she told me about what was happening on the farm.

"I have nearly every weekend off and rarely have to work past five in the afternoon," I wrote. "But the war rages on in both Europe and Asia, and men are constantly being sent overseas. I have no idea when I might be shipped out." This confirmed the wisdom of our decision to postpone wedding plans until after the war.

"White," my commanding officer said one day, "This Demonstration Regiment represents the best the Army has to offer in medical training." As we talked, he shared with me his conviction that it was most unlikely that any of the 20 of us would ever be assigned another duty. "I think we are here to stay for the duration of the war," he mused.

Chapter 18

WEDDING BELLS

As the days and weeks passed, I pondered my situation and my commanding officer's thoughts.

"Mardell, my love," my pen scratched, "it seems almost certain that the Demonstration Regiment will be in operation at Fort Knox until the war ends. What would you think of our marrying and your moving here to Fort Knox?"

I wish I could have seen her face when she read that letter! I wish I could have listened in on the discussions she had with her parents. All I know is that when she wrote back, she said, "The little church my dad helped build years ago, right near the center of town, would be a perfect place for our wedding."

Letters flew back and forth. I requested a furlough, and finally, the myriad details were complete. We set our wedding date for August 26, 1943.

"Honey," she wrote, "the war has created shortages of many things that usually accompany a wedding. Can you be satisfied with a very simple service—one without most of the usual trimmings?"

"Oh Precious, we could be married in your living room with nothing more than some flowers from your yard, and I would be thrilled just to claim you as my bride," I answered.

A few weeks before our wedding, I wrote to my dad and mentioned rather casually that it would be nice if he and his wife could be there for my wedding. To my utter surprise, he wrote back almost immediately that they planned to come!

Four days before the wedding, I boarded a train in Louisville and headed northwest toward Nebraska by way of Chicago. Per army orders, I traveled in full dress uniform. Two days later, the train thundered into Norfolk, Nebraska, a hub for trains coming from every direction. I changed to the north-south train for the final 125 miles north to Lynch and Mardell. We stopped at the second station in Norfolk to pick up passengers from the East and West. Some passengers got off, others boarded.

I chose a seat near the rear of the car. Stowing my bag and preparing to sit, my eyes fell onto a magazine the previous passenger had left behind.

I was just beginning to leaf through it when I sensed someone staring at me. I glanced up and saw an older couple looking my way. I perceived that they were trying not to stare, but they were definitely looking me over from head to toe. I lifted the magazine to cover my face and slouched down in the seat, but I could still feel their eyes on me. Not interested in conversation, I continued looking at the magazine, only to look up and see the couple standing in the aisle right beside me.

"Excuse me, soldier. Is your name Charles White?" the man asked.

As I searched his face, I swallowed hard and felt liquid beginning to gather around the corners of my eyes. The man responsible for my birth stood before me. My *father*! I didn't know whether to jump for joy or sit down and cry, whether to shake his hand or hug him. I stood, still staring at him, he stepped toward me, and we embraced. We hugged for a long time, but not nearly long enough to make up for all those years apart. There in that slow-moving train, just two days before my wedding, I met my real father for the first time in my remembrance! He and his wife had arrived in Nebraska the same day I did, had boarded this very train, and had recognized me from the pictures I had sent them! The snail-paced train seemed to move faster as we began to get acquainted.

Just as Mardell had warned, our wedding lacked many of the fluff and frills of a big wedding, but for me it seemed perfect in every way. A local girl marrying a GI brought neighbors from far and near to help celebrate the big event, so we had many guests whom I didn't even know. Mardell looked smashingly gorgeous to me in her lovely gown, and she told me that I looked "handsomer than ever" in my uniform.

I can't remember a single thing in the preacher's sermonette, other than that marriage was God's idea and that God performed the first wedding service. All I could think of was how lucky I was to be marrying Mardell!

When she handed her bouquet to her bridesmaid and I took her hands in mine, I felt a thrill surge through me. She was going to be my wife! God be praised! He'd led me to the most wonderful woman in the world!

When the minister asked me if I took this woman to be my wedded wife, I joyfully exclaimed, "I do!" We promised to love each other in good times and bad, in sickness and in health, "till death do us part," and I couldn't imagine a happier moment.

The wedding reception had to be simple. The war imposed rations on so many foods that Mardell's mom and helpers worked a miracle to create a reception at all. We spent most of our honeymoon right there at the farm, staying about a week after the wedding. We revisited the spot where I'd proposed to her, chatted with local friends, and just enjoyed being together with her parents. Soon the inevitable day arrived when we had to leave. My bride took my hand as I helped her onto the train to Louisville and Fort Knox. The war still raged around the world, and I must fulfill my duty.

I had rented a small apartment in Louisville and furnished it with the bare necessities. Before she found work Mardell transformed that little apartment into a "little heaven here on earth." I began my daily 35-mile commute to Fort Knox in a carpool, and Mardell soon found work in a large wholesale hardware company as a billing clerk. We settled into a joyous routine, working together to make lunches for both of us, doing the household chores, and just loving each other.

I spent most of my time at our field medical station. When no groups were scheduled, I would work in the dispensary. One such day, a serviceman called in sick. When I saw him in the waiting room, he seemed strangely familiar. *Who is he?* I asked myself, furrowing my brow. Mustache . . . facial scar. He saw the captain (a doctor) and then came to the treatment area. He handed me his records so I could carry out the treatment of pills, shots, or whatever the doctor had ordered. As our eyes met, I knew! Before me stood the master sergeant who had caused me so much grief in the pressroom a year or so earlier. The same moment I recognized him, he seemed to recognize me, and he became quite agitated, as if he were going to leave without his injection.

I returned quickly with the needle and asked him to roll up his sleeve for the shot. As he reached for his sleeve, I noticed that he was not wearing any emblems signifying his rank. I also noticed the unfaded spot where the large insignia of master sergeant had been removed. I wondered what had happened.

"How long have you been here?" his subdued voice broke the awkward silence.

"About a year," I answered, as I finished his shot.

"Oh." That was all he said, and he turned and left.

Curiosity nearly consumed me. *What had caused him to lose his rank? Why had he been demoted to buck private, the lowest rank in the army?* Later, I learned that a couple of weeks after my miraculous transfer from the printing plant to the medics, he had been playing a card game and had gotten involved in a drunken brawl, seriously wounding another serviceman. Since this was not his first offense, he spent six months in the stockade, had been reduced to the lowest rank in the army, and had been assigned to the infantry unit scheduled for overseas appointment. His unit had come for the mandatory training before embarking. I never saw or heard of him again, and I have always regretted that I did not say anything to him about Christ at that single meeting.

EARLY YEARS:

RIGHT: Charles's parents, Charles Lucas White and Emily Alice White, at their wedding.

FAR LEFT: Charles, about 2½, after his aunt nursed him back to health.

LEFT: Charles, about 3, with one of his foster father's goats.

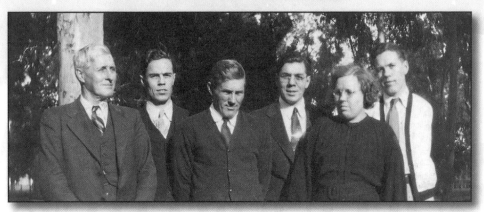

ABOVE: This is the first picture Charlie ever had of his brothers, sister, and dad. L-R: Dad, Ray, Harold, Lloyd, Bertha, and Wallace. Circa 1937.

Union College Days:

LEFT: Charlie, circa 1941.

BELOW: Union College, circa 1941.

LEFT:
Charles and Mardell at their wedding, August 26, 1943, Lynch, Nebraska. Charlie met his dad, Charles Sr. and his wife, Emma, for the first time the day before the wedding.

LEFT: Charlie and Mardell see Charles Sr. and Emma off as they return to Colorado after a visit.

BELOW: Charles and Mardell on their way back to Fort Knox, in Louisville, Kentucky, where he was stationed with the army, 1943.

ABOVE: Mardell's parents, Harold and Villiah Potter. Charlie considered them his parents after he and Mardell were married.

ARMY DAYS:

RIGHT: Fort Knox, 1943:
Charlie, third from right.

BELOW: Fort Knox, 1943:
Charlie, far right.

LEFT: Germany, 1944, 1945: All dressed up in uniform.

BELOW: Germany: Standing by a jeep.

LEFT: Germany, 6-10-45: Preaching from a "make-do" pulpit in a canvas church.

BELOW: Germany, 8-24-1945: Charlie's unit had taken over a monastery for a base near this bridge.

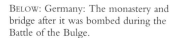

BELOW: Germany: The monastery and bridge after it was bombed during the Battle of the Bulge.

LEFT: Germany: Ruble at the base of the bombed bridge.

BELOW: Germany: Charlie surveys the damage from the top of the bridge.

Pastoring/Evangelism Days:

RIGHT: Charlie, Mardell, son Floyd, and daughter Ladonna. While pastoring in Beltsville, Maryland, Charlie built the school and classrooms.

BELOW: In 1959 Charlie did the preaching at meetings held in the Potomac Conference in Maryland. Elder Stimpson (on left) who had served with his wife served for many years in Pitcairn, and Albert Ellis (on right), were among the pastors from the surrounding area who had come to help with meetings.

RIGHT: 1964 found Charlie, Mardell, Floyd, and Ladonna in St. Louis Missouri, where Charlie conducted evangelistic meetings.

LEFT: Last church Charlie and Mardell helped build the church in Williamsburg, Virginia.

BELOW: Elder John Kozel, who had raised up this church before the Whites came, stayed on there until he retired.

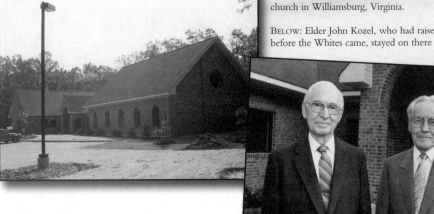

RETIREMENT AND BEYOND:

RIGHT: After retirement the Whites traveled to Seoul, Korea, in 1988 on a volunteer assignment Charlie was administrator of the service center. Soldiers came in from the nearby army base on weekends to enjoy the church service—and food that Mardell cooked from Friday through Sunday.

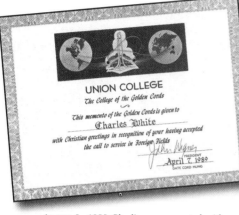

UNION COLLEGE
The College of the Golden Cords

This memento of the Golden Cords is given to

Charles White

with Christian greetings in recognition of your having accepted the call to service in Foreign Fields

PRESIDENT

April 7, 1989
DATE CORD HUNG

ABOVE: In 1989 Charlie was presented with the Union College Golden Cord award in recognition of his foreign service.

LEFT: Mardell and Charlie celebrated their sixty-first wedding anniversary in 2004.

RIGHT: Charles and Mardell's sixty-first wedding anniversary announcement appeared in *Southern Tidings*, October 2004.

Elder Charles and Mardell White celebrated their 61st wedding anniversary on August 26 in Collegedale, Tenn. They met at Union College in 1940. Charles has served as a pastor in seven conferences, administrator in two conferences, and full-time evangelist in three conferences. When the couple retired, they had served more than 50 years. They now enjoy their two grown children, four grandchildren, and two great-grandchildren.

LEFT: Charlie was the chaplain at National Health Care, an assisted living facility in Chatanooga, Tennessee. (Holding clock and record of clock). 6-30-2004.

BELOW: Charlie and Mardell on his 88th birthday at the Life Care Nursing Home, in Chatanooga, Tennessee. 9-1-2008.

Charlie passed away peacefully on 11-13-09.

Chapter 19

OFF TO WAR!

"Hey, White, have you heard that our Demonstration Regiment is going to be deactivated, and we're all going to be transferred to other places?" asked Jones, one of my fellow corpsmen.

"No way!" I replied. "You know how standard such rumors are for the army."

But not long afterward, we corpsmen somberly received the news that confirmed Jones's report. Officials at army headquarters in Washington had decided that our regiment had completed its assignment. "You will have a 21-day furlough to visit family and friends and/or settle your wives elsewhere before you are reassigned," we were told.

"Do you have any idea where we might be sent?" I asked our commanding officer.

"No, but in all likelihood, it will be somewhere overseas," he answered.

What a blow! Mardell and I would have waited to get married had we known this would happen. A glum atmosphere hung over us as we packed our belongings and boarded the train for Nebraska. She would live with her parents while awaiting my return.

"How can I tell you goodbye?" Mardell cried. She tried to be brave, but what thoughts must be going through her mind, for now she was five months pregnant with our first baby—and suddenly I was being taken from her! It didn't help matters when we listened to the news. Hundreds of American soldiers were dying every day—and now I was to join the soldiers lined up for the possibility of the same fate. Like many other soldiers all over the country, I had to tear myself from my wife's embrace and board the train headed back to Fort Knox.

"Just remember the 14 wonderful months we had together and trust our future to the Lord," I whispered as I gave her one last kiss.

Life at Fort Knox had taken a turn! Daily, men of all rank were being assigned to other units all over the United States. We all knew that whatever unit we were assigned to, we could soon expect to be sent either to

Europe or the Pacific. There were continual vacancies to fill, and I tried not to dwell on the fact that a vacancy meant another dead soldier, a grieving wife, a mourning family.

About a week after my return to Fort Knox my commanding officer handed me a sealed envelope. Hands trembling, I tore it open. "White, you are going to Hattiesburg, Mississippi, to join an army hospital preparing for overseas duty at an undisclosed location," I read. No other man from our unit accompanied me, and I did not know where I would be sent from Hattiesburg. Our small, tight-knit medical unit would no longer be together.

When I arrived in Mississippi, I learned that as a surgical technician, I would be part of a team consisting of two surgeons, one or two female nurses, and three to five enlisted technicians. Each day we practiced packing and unpacking all the surgical instruments and equipment needed for a functional field operating room. We set up operating rooms in tents and used plastic bodies to practice doing surgical procedures and handling the surgical instruments involved. Then we would pack everything up, only to unpack it again!

Our hospital unit consisted of 40 male officers (most of them doctors), 40 female nurses, and 250 noncommissioned men. Repeatedly trying to beat our previous time for packing and unpacking the equipment, our constant teamwork transformed us from a collection of individuals to a co-ordinated and close-knit team. Perhaps the fact that most of the doctors had been in civilian practice before the war helped—their attitude seemed more positive than that of the army-trained officers.

Just before we moved out from Hattiesburg, I received a telegram from my mother-in-law. "Congratulations! You are the father of a baby boy." She gave his weight and length, but I was too surprised by the fact that he had come six to eight weeks early to comprehend all the details.

What happened? Was the stress of having to move, the trauma of our forced separation too much for Mardell? I wondered. Being under orders for debarkation, no leave for any reason was granted. I telephoned and learned that she and the baby were just fine and were back at home.

The day before we boarded the train that would take us to the ship dock, I received another telegram. "Charles, your son is back in the hospital. Weight 5 lbs. 14 oz., premature lungs not strong enough to expel mucus."

Due to my impending move overseas, all phone calls were forbidden. What agony! *Oh God,* I pleaded, *please keep my son alive. Let him have strong lungs. How can I pray "Thy will be done" when I can't even be there to encourage Mardell or to hold my son?* But I had grown in my walk with Jesus enough that I wrenched out the words, "Thy will be done." And I wept. I cried for my son. I would never wish him the weak lungs I had struggled with for years. I willed him to be strong. But I had a job to do now, and I prayed for strength to push on.

One full train had been commissioned to transport everything needed for a 1,000-bed field hospital: tents for patient wards; cloth drapes, sterilizers, and myriad other surgical instruments; generators; sleeping quarters for all personnel; a large mess hall (dining room and kitchen); complete laundry facilities; a chapel tent; and a motor pool.

Wartime required keeping our movements as secret as possible. We pulled out under the cover of extreme secrecy and zigzagged our way toward Boston, which we found out only later was our classified port of debarkation. We could not talk with anyone outside of our unit along the way, and to ensure our cooperation, we were not even allowed off the train when it made its infrequent stops.

When we left the warm, humid Mississippi climate in mid-November, we had no idea that winter had already arrived in the Northeast. I had grown used to wearing lightweight cotton fatigues, feeling sweat on my skin even with that amount of clothing. We had been issued no winter uniforms, but because the train had heat, we didn't give our summer clothing a second thought. But when we pulled into a long, covered building in the Boston city harbor and saw the little whitecaps being whipped up by the wind, we looked at each other, down at our summer uniforms, back at each other, and groaned.

"Disembark the train in army formation," instructed the commanding officer. He took attendance not once, not twice, but three times, to be sure that no one had sneaked off the train during the trip. While we stood shivering, we saw other servicemen from local Boston camps busily removing all our hospital equipment and carrying it on board the ship. They wore overcoats, caps, and gloves, while we nearly froze in our cotton fatigues.

"You may talk with each other and you may smoke," shouted the commanding officer, "but stay in loose army formation." Talking and smoking were the last things on my mind. *Where can we find shelter from this cold wind?* I shivered as I tried to pull my collar up around my neck.

I finally gave up my search for shelter—any shelter—as we stood for over two hours shivering, waiting for the order to board the ocean liner. Finally, the order came. My white-knuckled hand reached down for the strap of my duffel bag, and I marched with the others toward the long gangplank at the far end of the mammoth vessel. On the gangplank we each had to show identification. Strangely, just before stepping onto the ship's deck, we had to go through the same identification process again. It took hours to get our unit of 330 soldiers and equipment loaded. Eventually, we were all issued warm clothes.

Several battalions of different skills and at least one more entire hospital unit also had to board, or had already done so. Small groups from six to a dozen were split from each unit and assigned to different locations all over the ship. Each of us was restricted to a limited area, so we did not get to learn much about the others who shared this trip with us. Most of us never saw anyone else from our own unit until we docked more than two weeks later.

Any hopes of a luxury liner were dashed! Stripped down for one purpose only—to transport service personnel and equipment overseas—even the name of the ship had been removed, along with any hint of luxury. Tiers of hammocks, five high, lined the walls of each of the small rooms constructed inside the massive ballroom. Men from various other units joined me in my "room." Forty of us were cramped into this one small space. It seemed that we would have a very "chummy" trip! After an eternity of getting the ship loaded, it began to vibrate gently and moved slowly away from the dock. We were on our way—destination unknown.

Shortly after departure, a navy man came to our door and asked, "Anyone for chow? Follow me."

We took a long walk, descending three flights of narrow stairs leading to a huge mess hall. Baby-stepping our way through the chow line, we received a metal tray topped with a substance that would serve as a meal, and then found a place at one of the many long, chest-high tables. Only these stand-up tables could handle the crowd of more than 5,000 people.

Once in open water, the ship zigzagged seemingly all over the Atlantic to avoid detection from lurking enemy ships or submarines. Our ship traveled in a convoy of several other vessels, spread out and always accompanied by smaller warships for protection. At least every hour, the entire convoy would change course. At dusk each night, all lights that could be seen on the outside had to be turned off, and we lived in total blackout, except for dim lights in each room.

My first trip to the mess hall proved to be my last! Soon after I arrived back at my assigned hammock, the meal I had enjoyed going down tasted much less enjoyable coming back up! I learned very quickly that I was a poor sailor. I crawled into my hammock and remained there, clutching my stomach, not able to eat or drink anything, for the majority of the trip.

"White, you look terrible," one of my buddies announced. "I'm going to call a doctor to come see you." When the unit physician examined me, he lamented that there was little he could do for me. "Try just a sip of water, 7-Up, or Coke," he counseled. "You need to get some fluids. You're already dehydrated." He gave me some pills that were supposed to relieve the nausea, and they helped a bit. I think I would have died right there in my hammock had it not been for my buddy calling the doctor.

About halfway across the Atlantic, the public address system crackled. "An enemy submarine has detected our convoy. Everyone to your assigned room." The ever-present knot in my stomach from the nausea tightened as I lay in my hammock facing the dingy ceiling above me. My roommates burst into the room and climbed into their hammocks. *Will our ship be torpedoed?* I whispered, "Oh God, if this is to be the end of my life, I claim Jesus' blood to cover all my sins. Prepare me for eternity with You."

Silence gripped my room—indeed the entire ship. Everyone waited to feel the impact of a torpedo. Time seemed to stand still. I hardly dared to breathe.

Finally, the loud speaker crackled again. "One of our troop ships traveling about half a mile away was attacked and sunk." We were never told the name of the ship or how many men were lost at sea. Swallowing hard and swiping my arm across my moist eyes, I thought about all the soldiers who had either been scorched to death or drowned in the cold, lonely waters of the Atlantic. My prayers certainly increased in fervency during the rest of our trip! I'm sure many others prayed, too. *Why them and not us?* I wondered. That question would frequently drum through my head during the remainder of the war.

After what seemed a lifetime our mighty ship slowed and dropped anchor in sight of South Hampton, England. It didn't really matter to me where we were—the dry land looked absolutely wonderful! It took me a few minutes to relearn how to walk on solid ground. We were transported by truck convoy to Wales, where we found an entire tent hospital set up overlooking the fabled White Cliffs of Dover.

I found a phone as soon as I could and called Mardell. Her soft voice began to still my anxious thoughts about her and our baby's welfare that had kept my mind rolling and heaving right along with the ship for so many days.

"He's doing fine," she assured me, giggling at my breathless stream of questions. "He seems perfectly healthy now." A huge burden rolled off my shoulders! "I'm doing well, too," she added. "Mom takes good care of both of us," she said. "Since I can't be with you, I'm glad I can be here with my folks."

The exorbitant cost of transcontinental telephone calls prohibited our talking very long, but what a relief it was to know that both Mardell and the baby were doing well! Promising to write as often as I could, I said goodbye and slowly replaced the receiver.

Immediately after arriving at our tent hospital we began practicing our skills. We had one problem, though: no actual patients. To compensate, most of our surgical teams were sent on temporary duty for one to two weeks to a large London field hospital, where seriously wounded soldiers evacuated from the battlefields in Europe arrived daily. More extensive surgery could be performed here than in the battlefield hospitals. Thus, we gained actual battlefield experience without being in a combat situation.

I had never seen such wounds before! Faces half blown off. Noses missing. One eye gone. Limbs torn off by hand grenades. Mangled bodies. I wept each day after my shift ended, partly because of the pain these victims suffered and partly because of their amazing courage. I learned very graphically that the will to live cannot be extinguished just because part of the body is missing.

"White, you are free to sightsee in London for three days before returning to your hospital unit," my commanding officer informed me after my two-week tour of duty in London. I guess it was a privilege, but this was at the height of Hitler's attempt to destroy England with almost constant bombing day and night. Both German aircraft and long-range missiles from the mainland of Europe kept the warning sirens wailing. Quite often I witnessed bombs landing in other parts of London, cringing at the resulting damage to buildings, streets—and people. I miraculously avoided the parts of the city receiving the heavy bombing, but to me, the war was no longer a distant drama played out on some stage overseas; I had been forced into a front-row seat!

Most of England's air defense had been destroyed, and most of its fighter planes had been shot down. It seemed inevitable that England, like most of Europe, would fall. But as I saw it, God's hand still reigned over the affairs of men, and England never fell to Germany.

About a week after we arrived back at our hospital unit in Wales, orders came to move out under cover of darkness in four days. By day, we continued our routines of make-believe care of imaginary patients. By night, we packed up all our gear. One evening, just after dark, we boarded trucks taking us by convoy to south England where we boarded a ship to cross the English Channel.

Happily, the trip proved uneventful. Knowing my experience in crossing the Atlantic, I took some sleeping pills before the ship left the dock. When I awoke the next morning, our ship had anchored offshore near Cherbourg, France. Only a couple of weeks before, this port had been the scene of one of the most intense sea and air battles of the entire war. Partially submerged ships and aircraft littered the harbor. The nearby city looked to be in total ruins. Since it was impossible to disembark here, we waited several hours to receive new orders. The entire time, planes flew over us like a great canopy to protect us from possible enemy attack.

We moved farther south, finally disembarking. January in France spells rainy season. Large trucks took us several slow hours away to the outskirts of a small French village, the name of which we never learned. Outside this village, about a mile from the road, we found large ward tents set up for sleeping quarters. We sloshed through the mud, carrying our duffel bags and personal items, in search of a bed and rest. The mess hall stood about another muddy mile away. For several days we waited for orders with nothing to do but slog through the muck to the mess hall three times a day.

Late one afternoon, our entire unit loaded onto a convoy of army trucks that traveled several miles over muddy, potholed roads to some railroad tracks out in the country. A European engine stood ready to pull the line of small freight cars, each with the sign "40 & 8." We soon learned that this meant 40 men or eight horses. The officers attempted to put 40 men or 40 nurses in each car. But with this many bodies jammed into a car, no one could lie down. There wasn't even room for everyone to sit on the bare straw-covered floor at the same time!

We were ordered back off the train and stood around in loose formation while our commanding officer argued with the French railroad official. Finally, the engine moved to a nearby sidetrack, and more cars were brought. With the additional cars we now had only 20 persons per car. Even this was rather crowded when we all lay on the floor. We stored our bags and most of our personal items in a separate car near the center of the long train. Five or six other cars carried our hospital equipment.

One car had a sign in English that read "Dining Car." Exactly like all the other cars, it was filled with hundreds of C rations and a large supply of drinking water in five-gallon containers. A dining car indeed!

"Attention! You are under strict orders to not throw anything—not even a small piece of paper—out of the cars as you travel." We learned that this was necessary to keep anyone from knowing that troops had passed over these tracks.

The train had no restrooms, so every four hours the train stopped and the doors slid open. The female nurses scurried into the woods on the left side of the train, and we men headed for the woods on the right side. The heavy bombing in France had destroyed much of the railroad system, making travel extremely slow. When we came to damaged tracks, the train stopped, and special troops riding in the first and second cars next to the engine jumped out and repaired the track so we could proceed across Northern France toward the Belgian border.

Finally, on day six of our uncomfortable train ride, we arrived just inside the Belgian border. We heard the sound of heavy artillery in the distance and felt thankful that, at least for now, no reconnaissance from the German side came to check out what we were doing. A large open field just off a main paved highway had been selected for us to set up our hospital. In a surprisingly short time we stood ready to receive patients.

Our encampment sprawled over a square mile, dominated by medical and surgical ward tents. There was also a tent for storing hospital supplies, a large chapel tent with an office and living quarters for the chaplain and his assistant, a kitchen tent with cooking stoves and the food supply, a tent housing generators to provide the power for lighting, a tent with several large washing and drying machines for the never-ending mountain of laundry, and personnel living quarter and shower tents. (The water shortage limited us to just one shower per week!) A motor pool lay to one side in anticipation of the logistic needs of a large hospital. The entire encampment was surrounded by an eight-foot fence topped with three strands of barbed wire, and armed guards stood at the only gate, regulating passage in and out 24 hours a day.

The battle line being less than 10 miles away, it proved easy to get the wounded to us. We quickly realized that we needed more medical and surgical ward tents to keep up with the swift-flowing river of wounded from the front lines.

Every one of our tents had a huge white square painted on the roof, with a large red cross in the center, identifying it as a hospital. The rules of the Geneva Convention forbade the enemy from bombing or strafing any hospital unit or vehicle on the road. Unfortunately, this rule was sometimes ignored, and we became victims of two attacks by enemy planes during the several months we were in the combat zone. Yet, miraculously, few were injured, and I myself sustained not even a scratch.

Although medics were forbidden from carrying armed weapons, we did have an attachment of infantry stationed next to us at all times. From my cot I could hear them on guard duty, walking back and forth, during the night. While I had no need to leave the encampment, I watched the infantry serving as guards at the gate, checking the identification of every person and vehicle entering or leaving.

As the battlefield shifted, we moved in order to stay nearby. I felt very thankful that we also had a large corps of army engineers who set up and dismantled the tents of our entire unit whenever we had to move. The only responsibility our hospital personnel had was that of packing and moving all the materials inside the tents.

"How fast do you think you can prepare for a move and then set up again?" our chief surgeon asked quizzically. From the time of receiving orders to move, we could normally wrap all the instruments, prepare all the linens in huge packs, prepare all the liquid disinfectants for safe travel, and be entirely packed up in 8 to 10 hours. After moving we could begin receiving new patients within 12 hours. We began to take real pride in shaving off even 10 to 15 minutes! With every move we not only became more efficient at moving but also crept closer to the heart of the battle.

Chapter 20

BEHIND ENEMY LINES

Before coming to Europe I had listened to the newscasts that kept American citizens informed about the horrors of D-Day and the invasion at Normandy Beach. As I listened to the news each evening after work, I shuddered. Now that I had arrived in Europe, the reality of war became more and more evident every day. Each time we moved, I saw buildings and entire villages devastated by bombs. Even historic churches, considered sacred for centuries, had been torn apart, with only partial walls remaining. As we drove through some villages, I didn't see a single human. *Where are the people who lived here?* I wondered. *Then again, how could they stay in such demolished homes?* A stray cat or dog with ribcage showing would limp by searching for some scrap to eat, attesting to the dire situation everyone suffered. *How can such evil continue? I hate war!*

Wounded soldiers flooded our tent hospital. Faces partially blown off, embedded shrapnel, legs dangling by threads of skin, disfiguring burns. Because of my specialized training, I worked as an operating technician from 1900 hours (7:00 p.m.) through the night until 0700 hours (7:00 a.m.) I prepared the instruments that would be needed for the surgeries, assuring that they were properly sterilized, and then I scrubbed in with the surgeon. I prayed for longer cases so I wouldn't need to scrub with the bristled brush and disinfectant soap quite so frequently! After donning my mask, sterile gown, and gloves I would help the surgeon into his sterile garb before surgery. Then, as the scrub nurse, I handed the needed instruments to the surgeon during surgery.

While training, my instructor had drilled into me, "You've got to pay attention to the surgery. You've got to learn what instruments the surgeon will likely need next and have them ready to slap into his hand when he holds out his hand—even before he asks for them. If you guess wrong, be prepared for hell!"

Now, the training was over and here I was assisting surgeons with lives in the balance. Working with the same surgeons day after day, I became pretty good at knowing what each one would want and having it ready for him. When I did guess wrong, Dr. Black, who always seemed to be having a bad day, would throw the instrument down in disgust and yell the name of the instrument he wanted, his outburst complete with an accompanying expletive. I preferred working with Dr. Jones. He never yelled, and he often thanked me at the end of the surgery for doing so well.

In addition to the wounded we also had a number of captured German soldiers and about 200 Polish refugees who attached themselves to us. The German POWs had to be kept under guard day and night, though many of them seemed quite content receiving three square meals a day! The Polish refugees proved helpful at keeping the garbage bins emptied and the camp area tidy.

"Must be a tough battle raging," Dr. Jones observed one day. "Look how dramatically the number of wounded soldiers has increased!" Three weeks later, after moving our encampment to keep up with the battle line, he wondered out loud, "What's going on now? We've been set up at this location for some time. Have you noticed that the number of wounded men has dropped?"

Uncertainty about the status of the war rested heavily on my heart. *Who was winning? What was the purpose of this war, anyway? What would happen if the war turned against us and we became prisoners of war?*

Intruding into my thoughts came a sudden order: "Take all of the records of patients, past and present, and all personnel records immediately to headquarters. Not one record is to fall into enemy hands." *What does that mean?* I wondered. *Are we about to be overrun? Are our troops failing?*

Then, very early one morning, just about the time I had completed my night's duty, we heard that the infantry assigned to our unit had been ordered to move out! We had no weapons and had come to rely on the small company of infantry patrolling the outer perimeter of our unit and guarding the German POWs. Now, they had been ordered to retreat and leave our unit unguarded. They did leave two soldiers for each shift to stand guard over the German POWs. *Would the Germans honor the Geneva Convention agreement that captured medical personnel must be treated better than a fighting soldier?* my mind asked over and over. We learned later that our infantry had been called in as reinforcements for the Battle of the Bulge, fought in the Ardennes forest on the German-Belgian border.

Our hospital again lay alongside a major highway. It was paved, and it provided exceptionally good connections with the other units. Thickly forested hills surrounded us, with snow lying heavily on tree boughs. Had it not been wartime, I would have thought the scene fitting for a picture postcard. Looking at the scenery was one thing, but being out in it was another. The cold that January of 1945 bit through my heavy overcoat as I slogged through 18 inches of snow to and from work. In the short time it took to run from my tent to the surgery tent my hands would turn to ice, and it felt like every ounce of blood had frozen in my body!

During the height of the battle, we felt the ground shake beneath us as we heard the approach of German tanks. They had mounted a counterattack and were pushing our own troops backward in a fast retreat. As the motorized section of the German army neared our hospital area, a strange thing happened. Their vehicles, followed closely by hundreds of armed foot soldiers, passed by on the right and left sides of our unit, completely surrounding us. We were behind enemy lines! We held our collective breath as we watched rank after rank of German soldiers march or run past our unit. Yet, not one of them came into our area, even though we had no infantry guarding us!

The entire time we were behind enemy lines, not one of our Americans could leave for any reason, and of course no new patients could be brought to us. Yet the Germans left us alone! German planes roared directly overhead daily, but they chose to honor the Geneva Convention guidelines. The red crosses painted on the top of our tents, together with God's miraculous care, protected the 1,500 wounded or sick servicemen and 350 doctors, nurses, camp cooks, and other service personnel.

As a frontline hospital, we carried only a few days of food rations. Being entirely cut off from any supply or contact, we wondered how long we could hold out. "You will be served only two meals a day," our commanding officer announced one day. "The cooks have advised me that our food rations are low, and of course, no replacements can be delivered as long as we are behind enemy lines." The variety of meals also suffered, but no one, either patients, personnel, or refugees, went hungry. "O God," I whispered each day, "Continue to protect us, and please deliver us." No one knew how long the German troops would leave us alone or how long our food supply would last.

One blustery day, we felt the ground tremble once again as German heavy ammunition tanks thundered by. But something was different. The sound seemed to be going in the direction from which it had come. *Could it be?* I thought excitedly. Yes! They were retreating! We were too far from the road to see the soldiers, but we could hear their hobnailed boots pounding on the pavement as they beat a fast retreat, following their motor units. With joy I thanked God for His miraculous care. Soon, our small contingent of infantry came back, and our activities returned to a more normal schedule—as normal as possible being so near the battle line. With the Germans gone, the streams of wounded soldiers and supplies began to flow in once again.

In this freezing landscape the Battle of the Bulge, one of World War II's bloodiest, claimed the life of one of our unit's captains. Nineteen thousand other American soldiers died in that battle, and almost 24,000 were captured. We learned later that even though the German offensive was a total surprise, nowhere did the American troops give ground without a fight. Our brave troops, struggling through the snow and subfreezing temperatures, fought bravely, preventing the Germans from achieving their interim objective.

Chapter 21

YOU WANT *WHAT?*

One Saturday night a couple of weeks after the Battle of the Bulge, the commanding officer strode into the surgery area where I was assisting the surgeon.

"White," he said in a measured tone, "don't turn around, keep working. I have a request for you. I want you to fill in at the Sunday services tomorrow. Our chaplain suffered serious wounds from exploding shrapnel yesterday while on a mission. He will be unable to hold services, so I want you to fill in for him tomorrow. I don't have a replacement for you here in surgery tonight, so you'll have to continue your duties throughout the night."

The surgeon stopped working on his patient momentarily, nodding for me to turn and talk with the commanding officer. "Sir, I am not a preacher," I protested. I have had only three semesters of college training."

He held up his hand to stop me. "White, we have no one else. Our records show you to be the only one in our entire unit who has had *any* training toward the ministry. We have sent word to headquarters requesting a new chaplain, but we have no idea when he will arrive. I am sure you will do fine until the replacement arrives. The first service tomorrow is at 0900 hours [9:00 a.m.]." With that, he turned and left the tent.

I turned around and nodded to the surgeon that I was ready to proceed, but my mind started racing. *What can I preach about? Can I remember any really good sermons I've heard?* I'm not sure I functioned as a surgical assistant as well as I should have the rest of the night, as my mind spent the rest of the shift darting between sewing up the patient in front of me, to having to preach the next day, to pleading with God for wisdom.

I had time between the end of the shift and the first service to change from my surgery scrubs into my military uniform. Entering the chaplain's office to see what he had scheduled, to my dismay, I had five services back to back! I took my Bible and prayed some more. The words I spoke that day have faded, falling beyond the reach of my memory, but I'm sure I walked up to stand before those servicemen on trembling legs! It didn't help that the colonel walked in and sat on the front row, an expectant smile on his face!

Amazingly, during the first few minutes of the first service, my knees stopped quivering and my paralyzed tongue broke free. Clearly, God had prepared me for this very moment by teaching me to think on my feet while a trainer at the Demonstration Regiment.

At the end of the service, the colonel walked up to me and said, "Good work, White. And you said you aren't a preacher? You can't fool me!"

The next day, the commanding officer sent for me. "White, I need you to carry on with all the duties of the chaplain until a replacement can be found. Unfortunately, I have no one to replace you in surgery, so you will need to fill that position, too."

For the next several weeks, I worked in the operating room from 7:00 p.m. until 7:00 a.m. and then all day as chaplain, conducting five services each Sunday and visiting all the wounded admitted to our hospital. What seemed the very minute I reached complete exhaustion, an operating room technician replacement arrived, and I was officially commissioned as a "battlefield chaplain."

Steve Willis, the chaplain's assistant, drove the jeep and stocked the trailer that we pulled when we went out on missions. We carried candy, biscuits, cookies, cigarettes, and Bibles. Often our men out on the front lines had not had a candy bar for days. I carried the lovely Bible that I'd received my first "real Christmas" in my front shirt pocket, and it seemed to inspire some men to accept the pocket Bibles we offered. Many men seemed to treasure the Bibles even more than the sweets.

"White," the commanding officer said one day, "I have sad news. Our chaplain died during the night last night. Until a replacement arrives—and I seriously doubt that one will—you'll be our chaplain." For the next six months I served as the chaplain for our hospital unit, and I made it a point to visit every single person admitted to our unit.

Many centuries ago, the prophet Isaiah wrote, "And it shall come to pass, that before they call, I will answer; and while they are yet speaking, I will hear" (Isaiah 65:24). God heard my desperate cries for inspiration, strength, and wisdom to serve as a chaplain, and His promise proved just as valid and true in battle-torn Germany as it had thousands of years ago.

The war seemed to be grinding to an end. Yet, in spite of this, some of the fiercest battles had yet to be fought. Each day I received information about where the various troops were stationed within a radius of about 20 miles. No longer behind enemy lines, but very near the fighting, Willis and I went on missions to these troops. Sometimes we started after dark and kept going late into the night. Behind bombed-out tanks, in basements, behind a bunker, in trenches—wherever I could find a few soldiers—I offered communion (that was a rule of the army), prayed with them, offered a brief inspirational talk, and then we gave them whatever items we had with us that they requested. These gatherings had to be held in total darkness and as quietly as possible, and one man would always stand guard to watch for enemy soldiers. Many nights, I conducted as many as 12 such meetings.

On one such mission our service was interrupted by the whine of a shell approaching. Being in the basement, we had nowhere to hide. The shell was a dead hit, and one of our soldiers was killed instantly, his head partially blown off. As blood and human body parts spattered the basement, my first thought was, *Why him and not me?* Several other soldiers received major wounds, one bleeding profusely from his head, and another from a seemingly fractured arm. The soldiers became frantic, some screaming, some praying aloud. I didn't want the noise to attract enemy soldiers, so I shouted, "Hush! Be quiet!" Our sentry soldier also motioned with his finger to his lips to be quiet, and the panic subsided.

With my medical training I immediately turned to the soldier with the head wound. "Someone please help me," I whispered urgently. "Press this bandage firmly against his head to stop the bleeding." Then I turned my attention to the man with the fractured arm. "Can you wiggle your fingers?" I asked, peering into his frightened eyes. He tried but groaned with the pain. "Get me something to make a splint—anything firm, and long enough to go from his shoulder to his fingertips," I instructed. One of the men found a splintered piece of wood from the building's roof, and we tied it in place with several bandages that I carried in my first aid kit.

"Now, let's get these men ready for evacuation as soon as some medics arrive," I said. I quickly prepared a shot of morphine for the man with the fracture. The other soldier's bleeding had slowed, and he wasn't groaning in pain.

I wondered what I should do about the dead soldier. What should I say? Everyone realized he was dead, so there was no point in trying to resuscitate him. Capitalizing on the moment, I urged each GI to accept Jesus as his Savior so that, should his life end, he would be right with God.

One night, after ministering to several groups of men, Willis and I began our journey homeward. Traveling without headlights to avoid detection, we heard the familiar whine of another approaching shell. Before Willis could bring the jeep to a stop, it shook violently from the impact. Instinctively, I ducked below the dashboard. The shell hit our trailer and wrenched it completely from the jeep, stopping us dead in our tracks. I expected to hear broken glass crashing, but amazingly, the windows remained intact. As the dust began to settle, I straightened from under the dashboard and looked over at Willis.

"Are you hurt?"

Slowly Willis shook his head. "I don't think so." Shaken, but miraculously unharmed, it took a few minutes before his hands stopped trembling. We tried to open the trailer door, but it was jammed shut. "I hate to leave the trailer here with all the supplies," I mumbled. "Won't the Germans have a feast if they can manage to open the door!"

"Willis," I asked. "Do you believe in miracles?"

"I'm not sure, sir," he replied. "I never did believe in God, and I have never been a churchgoer . . ." His voice trailed off in uncertainty.

"Well," I said quietly, "you've just experienced a miracle. God has something important for both you and me to do."

"Don't preach, Chaplain," he pleaded. "I can't help listening as you talk to our boys, and I did take one of the Bibles—I've started reading it. But just give me time." Even though the jeep itself had remained unharmed, we had to abandon the trailer. We traveled a bit more slowly back to base in silence. I was silently praising God that He was already working on Willis' heart, and he was apparently deep in thought, as well.

When our unit received orders to move, this time I didn't have to help pack and unpack the operating room. But having never packed up the chaplain's office, it took me quite a while, and I appreciated Willis' help. This move took us closer to the battle line again. Instead of setting up tents, we moved into an abandoned monastery. Several three-story buildings covered many acres, amazingly showing no battle scars! A miraculous find, it served our needs very well.

Eight nuns had remained at the monastery, and they became official prisoners of war. We settled them comfortably in quarters on the third floor of one of the buildings. As POWs, they ate from our supplies. They never attempted an escape, which led me to wonder if they rather enjoyed the security of their situation.

The rest of the third floor and the entire second floor served as quarters for all our nurses. How they rejoiced to be out of tents and into an undamaged building again! The first floor and basement served as quarters for the male officers. Sadly, most of the men completely ignored the army rule forbidding them to fraternize with the Germans, preferring to find rooms—and female companionship—in the nearby village.

The main monastery soon filled with patients, and it became necessary to set up large ward tents in the surrounding area. Having no adequate place in the buildings for the mess hall, we used tents for meals once again.

A peaceful Catholic chapel in the monastery with three large stained glass windows proved to be the most enjoyable and comfortable place for religious services of any setting we had experienced. This idyllic setting offered no hint that I was poised for one of the most heart-pounding experiences of my life.

Chapter 22

LOST IN THE NIGHT

Each evening, Willis and I visited troops out in the field within a 20-mile radius of our unit. "Out in the field" meant that the men had no tents, only their C rations for food, and were under the command of their chief officer until a skirmish had accomplished a desired goal, or until they were relieved by another unit and allowed to return to the main outpost.

One evening, I met with Willis at 1700 hours (5:00 p.m.) and prepared to leave.

"We have five outposts to visit this evening," I said as I climbed into the passenger seat. "If all goes well, we should be back by midnight. If things don't go so well, it'll be later, as you well know." He returned my quick grin.

"Everything's ready to go," Willis reported. "The trailer is stocked with all the standard C rations, cigarettes, candy, Bibles, and stuff. I serviced the jeep, so it's good for another 10,000 miles. I even got a new chaplain's flag and have attached it to the front bumper." He motioned toward the front of the vehicle. Normally, even enemy soldiers honored the chaplain's flag and didn't shoot at us—provided they could see the flag!

Knowing it would be cold after dark, I grabbed my overcoat and suggested to Willis that he take one along as well.

Our hospital unit lay about two miles off the Great Highway that Hitler had stretched across Germany, its four lanes bridging raging rivers and deep valleys. Willis and I used this highway whenever possible, always planning to head back to the hospital unit no later than midnight to be sure to arrive at the admission tent before 0530 hours (5:30 a.m.) when the battlefield wounded began to arrive.

The jeep purred along for some distance before we came to a long bridge over a deep ravine, along the bottom of which flowed a river filled with water from the spring rains and from snow still melting in the mountains. I thought to myself, *I'm surely thankful that this bridge hasn't been bombed out. Without it, we wouldn't be able to reach some of our troops.* We had to be more careful once we reached the other side of the bridge, because we were in enemy territory. Willis slowed the jeep so we could keep a watch for German patrols.

Each outpost differed from the next. Some were trenches where our men had dug in to avoid enemy fire until they could make another advance. Some were groups of army units hiding wherever they could find a basement, an abandoned building, or a barn. While each location differed dramatically, they all had certain things in common. Soldiers commonly asked, "Do you have candy?"

"Sure do! What kind do you want?"

"Have you got any Tootsie Rolls? I need a chocolate fix!"

Another would ask, "How about Camel cigarettes? I'm clear out of smokes."

We tried to anticipate what they would ask for and carry replenishments. We always carried a large supply of small Bibles, and a surprising number of the men requested them.

Our last outpost that night was an old barn. The men had built a small fire inside, and its warmth welcomed us along with the weary soldiers. I held a communion service with those who wished to participate, and all of them seemed anxious to join in when I offered prayer. Just about the time I said "Amen," all heads looked up at the sound of a huge plane flying over, not directly overhead, but close, followed by an explosion. It sounded like the bomb was dropped a couple of miles away, yet we could feel a slight tremor under our feet.

"I hope they didn't get any of our men," someone worried. A shudder surged down my spine as I thought of the terrible cost of war. One of the men let out a low moan. I looked his way in the dark and asked if he needed anything.

"Do you have a Bible?" he asked softly.

Willis handed me one, and I gave it to the man. He held it for a moment, saying nothing. Then he said quietly, "My buddy got blown to bits this afternoon, and I've . . . I've got to find something to help me through." His voice broke as I stepped over beside him and drew him close. His whole body began shaking as I lowered him to the ground and sat beside him. He leaned his head into my shoulder and wept like a baby for several minutes. I remembered how Mardell had wept on my shoulder under the elm tree the day I asked her to marry me. *Very different circumstances,* I thought. I felt that I needed to sit and just listen to him talk for as long as he needed, yet I also knew that if we didn't start back to base soon, we wouldn't arrive in time for the new admissions.

"Try reading Psalm 23. You might also find comfort from Psalm 91," I soothed. "Can you remember those chapters? Psalm 23 and Psalm 91," I repeated, hoping the chapter numbers would stick in his mind.

He nodded.

I asked him if he would like me to pray with him before I left, and he whispered, "Yes."

"Father God," I began, "You know the horrors of war. Please comfort this man as he tries to sort out his thoughts. Thank You for sparing his life, and lead him to Jesus, I pray. Amen."

He paused a minute with his head bowed. Then I said, "Young man, when you get back to base, come and see me in the chaplain's tent and we can talk some more." I felt frustrated that I couldn't take the time to really minister to his deepest needs, but I also knew that we *had* to get back to the hospital.

Willis and I bade the men good-bye and headed for the jeep. The cold breeze made me catch my breath when we stepped outside, and I was grateful for the overcoat I was wearing. The area where the vehicle was parked made getting out tricky. Willis had to back the jeep and trailer several times, but eventually we were out on the road and headed toward "home." I looked over at Willis just as he stifled a yawn. "You tired too?" I asked.

"Yeah—just a bit."

We traveled in silence very slowly and without headlights since we were behind enemy lines. The war had not been kind to the roads connecting to the Great Highway, and only a sliver of moonlight in an overcast sky spilled onto the path in front of us. But Willis expertly swerved around dislodged boulders, dodged the biggest potholes, and avoided the craters from exploding bombs. Finally, we bounced onto the Great Highway, and I breathed a sigh of relief. We had driven that road just a few hours before—when it had been totally free of damage.

We'd driven in silence for about five minutes when I heard a voice inside my head that commanded, "Stop!" It was as distinct to me as if I'd heard a thunderclap through the treetops. I glanced over at Willis to see if he'd heard it, but he didn't flinch, and his eyes remained on the road ahead. The darkness of the German night made the order seem important, yet inside the army jeep with Willis, I doubted my own senses and didn't say or do anything.

Willis leaned forward, urging his eyes to see farther into the night. With jaw clenched and mouth stretched into a thin line, his white-knuckled fingers held the steering wheel in a death grip. Tension filled every corner of the jeep.

"Stop!" Again the word reverberated in my head. I squinted, searching Willis' face for a reaction. Again, he seemed to have heard nothing. The voice seemed ominous, and the night's darkness oppressed me. I took a couple of deep breaths to still my thumping heart, but again I said nothing.

"*Stop!*" This time I couldn't ignore it. I knew I had to act.

"Stop!" I commanded.

Willis jammed on the jeep's brakes and looked over at me for an explanation.

"I don't know. I just know I heard this voice in my head commanding us to stop. I heard it three times." He probably thought I was crazy. "Let's get out and check," I said as I stepped out on the ground.

I couldn't explain why, but I dropped to my hands and knees and started crawling forward. Willis followed my example. I inched along, my hands feeling the rough pavement. Suddenly, the feel of the pavement disappeared and my hand dropped into an open space. *Some pothole!* I thought. I lay down on my stomach and reached my other hand out in front of me. It also dropped below the level of the road, and I realized that I could swing both hands in a wide arc without touching anything. *Nothing! Some huge pothole!* I turned to Willis. "I can't feel anything in front of me," I whispered. "Go slow!"

He gasped. "There's nothing out there! Where did the road go? I can't see a thing ahead of me!"

The cold wind, while not violent, blew steadily, and just then it pushed the clouds away from the moon. In the dim light we saw a surreal, ghastly sight. The moonlight flickered off of torn bridge girders and blasted pieces of metal, and a hundred feet below, it danced here and there off of ripples in the river!

"A bombed-out bridge! That's what that last plane did!" Willis sucked in his breath and put his hand on my shoulder. He was shaking like a leaf in the wind "We almost drove straight to our death!" he exclaimed. I could hear his teeth chattering.

Because I was older and "in command," I knew I must remain calm. I also knew that we were still in enemy territory until we reached the other side of the ravine, and now there was no easy way to cross.

"We'll have to walk along the cliff until we can find a way to ford the river on foot," I said, trying to sound composed. "We'd better stuff our pockets with everything we can carry." As quietly as I could, I opened our trailer's door and began preparing for—for who knew what! I always carried a penlight in my shirt pocket on our excursions to visit the troops. Reaching for it, I shone it into the interior of the trailer. We stuffed our pockets with candy bars, biscuits, cookies—anything we could use for food. I also stuffed our maps, orders, and all other identifying papers into my overcoat pockets.

"Help me disable the motor," Willis said. "I want to make this jeep as useless as possible in case the enemy finds it. He opened the hood, and I shone my penlight so he could remove the wires from the spark plugs. With a pen knife that he carried in his pocket, he was able to remove the distributer cap, and he pitched it and the wires as far out into the black hole in front of us as possible.

Then we turned to the task of finding an alternate way across the river. I could hear the spring run-off in the river below. "If we follow the stream a ways, the cliff may drop far enough down that we can find a way to wade across," I said. *But should we go to the left or the right?* I breathed a prayer for guidance and took off to the left. Willis followed me. Almost immediately, we were plunged into a forest with thick underbrush. As silently as we could, we picked our way along the bank high above the stream, but any thought of rapid progress tumbled over the cliff and splashed into the water far below.

My penlight helped us around the most difficult spots, but I used it sparingly in order to keep the batteries from running down—and to avoid being seen by German soldiers.

"Ouch!" Willis groaned, as he sank to the ground between a bush and tree trunk.

"What's the matter?"

"I turned my ankle. Stepped on something . . . maybe an exposed root." He was breathing hard, and I could tell he was in pain. "I think it'll be OK," he grunted. Just let me rest for a minute or two."

I eased my way over to him. "Which leg did you injure?" I asked, bending over him.

"My right," he said.

I turned on the penlight long enough to locate his right leg. Then I felt all along his ankle. "Does it hurt when I squeeze?" I asked.

"No." I turned his foot slightly inward. "Does that hurt?"

"No." I turned it gently outward. "How about the other way?"

"No."

"OK," I said. "I think you'll be alright. But lean on me as a crutch." Our progress even slower, we limped along for several minutes.

"Let me try it alone," he said in a determined tone.

He gingerly took a few steps. "It'll be OK. My high-topped boots give quite a bit of support."

We picked our way through the underbrush in silence for several minutes, making sure we could hear the river on the right—otherwise we'd *really* get lost. The clouds had slid in front of the moon again, leaving the thickly-forested hillside in inky blackness. Groping in the darkness, we had to be very careful lest a low branch catch us in the eye.

The sound of a dog barking no more than 100 feet away froze us both in our tracks. A dog meant people, and the last thing we needed was to encounter Germans! I was sure Willis could hear my heart pounding, though I had to tell myself that, since I couldn't hear his, he surely couldn't hear mine. After trying not to breathe for what seemed like 10 minutes and hearing nothing more, we started forward again, doubly focused on making as little noise as possible. We also changed our direction a bit toward the river to avoid coming any nearer the dog.

After what seemed like an hour of picking our way through thick underbrush, sometimes falling, sometimes scraping our shins against rocks, I paused. "Where are we?" I asked.

"I haven't a clue!" Willis breathed. We are *really* lost!"

Suddenly, the clouds shifted and a shaft of moonlight faintly highlighted a large barn just ahead. Again we froze because a barn meant people.

Chapter 23

TRAPPED

The cold night air combined with my raw nerves caused me to regard the barn as a very welcome hideout where we could warm up a bit. Circling the barn twice, we approached the door cautiously. I listened intently to see if I could hear any sounds of human activity inside. Nothing.

Warily we inched the door open far enough to squeeze inside, then closed it behind us. I briefly shone my penlight around the barn and saw a ladder leading to a second-story loft. The smell of hay lured me up the ladder and into the hayloft. Willis followed.

I felt it was safe enough to shine the penlight again and saw a big mound of hay. Cobwebs hung from the roof's beams and half-covered a small window. As soon as I saw the window, I quickly turned off the light. "Burrow into the hay," I whispered to Willis. It's good insulation. You can make yourself a sort of cave in the hay, lie down, and get some rest. Better yet, let's make a cave big enough for both of us."

We quickly clawed out chunks of hay and threw them to the side. It took us several minutes to create a hay cave big enough for two. Crawling into our cave, we pulled hay over our entrance and eased ourselves onto our bed of hay, aching for sleep.

Suddenly, I sat bolt upright. I sensed that Willis had heard what I heard because he jerked upright, too. The barn door had been shoved open, and the sound of loud joking filtered up to our loft. The aroma of coffee mixed with campfire smoke soon followed, and I realized that German soldiers were taking a break directly beneath us! Ardently I silently prayed, *Oh Father, don't let them come up here. Let this just be their break.*

Eternity passed. Finally, I could hear the men stomping out the fire, and the barn door squeaked open again, then closed. The sound of their boots fading brought silence back to the barn.

"Whew!" Willis whispered. "I was sure scared!"

"Me, too," I admitted. "And I prayed that God would keep them down below."

After a thoughtful pause Willis whispered, "You really do believe in God, don't you?"

"After all I've been through—yes, I sure do. I know He lives and that He watches over me. Look at the bridge thing. I know it was God's voice commanding us to stop. And think of the time the trailer was blown from our jeep, and the time a shell killed one of our men but didn't harm either you or me. Those had to be miracles."

"Do you read the Bible?" Willis queried.

"Absolutely, I do. How do you think I could pass Bibles out to the men if I didn't read it myself? Now, let's try to get some sleep. We really can't go anywhere in the dead of night."

Wondering how God was going to work this one out for us, I slipped into halting half-dreams. I was enfolding Mardell in a long embrace. Then I was holding my son, who was now nearly a year old, rocking him in my arms. But whose were the other voices? What were they saying? Suddenly my eyes opened, and the voices continued. They were real, and they were German.

Dust on the barn window strained the sunlight penetrating our cave. I looked over at Willis, who was beginning to stir. I touched him lightly and whispered, "Shhh." I heard the voices drawing closer. Women's voices. I carefully crawled to a spot where I could peer between some boards. *Farm women.*

They entered the barn's lower floor. Oblivious of our presence, they laughed and talked, and I heard the clank of garden tools as they gathered the supplies for their day's work. Soon the barn door creaked again, and the women left. Peering out the window, we watched them fan out in different directions.

"Do you think we ought to stand watch at the window?" Willis asked. I think we could outrun the women if we attempt an escape."

"I think it might be a good idea to watch for a while, but what if they started shouting at us if we started running? Would that attract German soldiers?" I asked.

We decided to watch through the cobwebs from our upper window and plan our escape for later that day. I ate a few biscuits and munched on a cookie while I took my turn at "standing guard" at the window.

Alas! Around noon, rather than leaving, as we had hoped they would, the women returned, unaware that two frightened American soldiers hid in the loft above them. I could smell their sauerkraut and wondered what else they were eating before they returned to the field. My stomach growled in protest. Cookies and candy just didn't fill me!

"Let's be ready to leave as soon as they finish and head for their village," I suggested.

They returned as the afternoon sun grew old in a deep, blue sky. Storing their tools, they closed the barn door behind them and left. Now was our chance!

When the last woman walked out of view, we scurried down the ladder and opened the barn door. Just as we were about to step outside, we heard the sound of an engine. We had been in combat long enough to recognize the difference between American and German vehicles.

"German!" we both gasped at once.

The jeep turned into the driveway that led directly toward us. We hurriedly shut the door and scrambled back up the ladder, retreating to the hayloft. Peering through the window, we saw four German soldiers, each armed with a rifle with a fixed bayonet, jump from the vehicle. We ducked our faces behind the window frame. Since neither of us could speak German, we couldn't understand what they were saying. From their voices, we guessed they were just outside the barn door.

The smell of smoke intertwined with the aroma of food ascended up the ladder, and the clatter of metal spoons against metal mess kits confirmed that they were eating supper. As we waited breathlessly, the sun went down and the stars came out. Surely they'd drive back to their camp after their meal—but no. Beams of light from their flashlights began to dance around the walls, and we burrowed deep into the haystack just in case they should climb up into the loft.

Their talking and laughing gradually faded and was eventually replaced by heavy breathing.

"Do you think we could sneak past them?" Willis whispered.

"Remember those bayonets? I don't know if all of them are sleeping or if one of them is standing guard," I replied. "I'm staying put till they're gone."

Although the Germans had no idea that two American soldiers were trapped above them, God knew. In my head, I recited some of His promises of care and deliverance. And how I prayed! Even though I knew God's angels protected us and I felt an inner peace, it was still hard to sleep.

The next morning, even before I smelled the bacon, I could hear it sizzling over their camp stove. They joshed while eating, then packed and drove away. We had just reached the ladder, ready to attempt our escape, when we heard the women's voices. Again we hid in the hay and waited. Tools collected, the women dispersed to their various fields as we watched from our window.

"What shall we do, Chaplain?" His question sounded more like a weary statement.

"I'm hoping that if we wait till we're sure the women are all working, we can escape this barn," I replied.

"But what if someone sees us?"

"Well," I said, "what other option do we have? After dark, soldiers might camp downstairs again. Even if they don't, we would have trouble seeing. A couple of days ago we got lost in the dark, remember?"

Quietly we discussed our plight, trying to decide what the best course of action might be. Just then we heard children's voices. Listening carefully, we could distinguish only two, and as we cautiously peered out the window, we spied two young boys, probably 10 to 12 years old.

Were they friends or foes?

Chapter 24

CAN WE TRUST THEM?

The two German lads neared the barn. One was quite a bit taller than the other. Though shorter, the younger lad seemed to be the leader, walking ahead of the taller boy with an assured sort of swagger. Both were skinny and wore patched pants and somewhat ragged shirts. Although it was cool, neither wore a jacket. The leaves and twigs in their blonde hair suggested that they'd been exploring in the forest.

Our window of opportunity was small, so I made a bold decision. I crawled down the ladder and motioned for Willis to follow me. Just as the boys opened the barn door, I said, "Hi boys. Would you like some candy?"

Even by the dim light in the barn, I could see their eyes widen with terror at the sight of two uniformed American soldiers. The younger one started to cry out, but clapped his hand over his mouth. The taller one jerked around as if to flee, but the shorter one grabbed his arm and held on tightly. Both lads swept the barn with their eyes, then focused on us. They seemed frozen in place.

I deliberately brushed off some of the hay from my uniform and picked off some of the longest pieces from Willis's shoulders. Then both Willis and I held out a candy bar in our hands while we motioned for them to come. They eyed us warily, looking first at me, then Willis. We finally convinced them by sign language that we wouldn't hurt them, that we had no guns, and that the candy was for them. The shorter lad moved first. Taking a deep breath of air, he stepped forward and took the candy bar from my hand. The taller boy followed, snatching the candy bar from Willis' hand. Eagerly, both boys tore off the candy wrappers and ate the candy in almost a single gulp. They smacked their lips, enjoying the sweet luxury.

"The poor kids probably haven't had any candy since the war began," I said aloud to Willis. The boys tilted their heads at me questioningly.

I motioned to the candy, then to my uniform, and pointed in the direction I thought our hospital unit lay. Willis joined me in motioning with his hands, making walking steps with them in front and us following behind. We gave each boy another candy bar, and then Willis, who knew a few words of German, began to try to converse with them. He urged them to tell nobody about us, to find the American line, and then to come back and tell us where it was. He promised them more candy if they returned without telling anyone.

What did we have to lose? We would surely end up as POWs whether the boys led us to the Germans or . . . wandered around on our own not knowing where we were going. If we followed the boys, at least we had a chance that they would take us up on our offer. We decided to risk our lives with these two lads.

The boys looked at each other and once again scanned the barn. When they were sure no one else was there, they turned and ran from the barn. We watched in dismay as they headed for the nearby garden plots where they talked with two of the women. Neither the boys nor the women looked our way, and we felt assured that they had not reported our presence. The boys headed off through the woods from whence they had come and disappeared out of sight. All we could do now was wait—and pray!

When we noticed the women coming toward the barn, we retreated quickly to the hayloft. Eating their lunch just beneath us, they laughed and talked with each other, again unaware of our presence. The aroma of sausages and sauerkraut made my stomach growl. After putting away their lunches, they gathered their tools and returned to their gardens. Time dragged by. Should we attempt our escape and take our chances of getting away? Just about the time we had decided the boys had deserted us and had maybe even reported us to enemy headquarters, the women came back to the barn. It took them a while to put their tools away, and they seemed in no hurry to head down the dusty road toward the nearby village.

We could hear the occasional stuttering of gunfire in the distance and decided to head in that direction as soon as the women were out of sight. We stepped outside the barn and were listening carefully to try to determine whether we could detect any other human sounds. Just then we spotted the boys coming out of the woods toward us.

This time, each boy was wearing a light jacket over his shirt. Still unsure what the boys might do, we stepped back into a dark corner of the barn and waited for them to enter. We wanted to make sure they had not brought a German soldier to take us captive. We heard them slowly open the barn door and enter alone. We stepped out from the shadows, smiled, and said, "Hi." The first thing they wanted was the candy. We gave each of them two bars and promised more as soon as we found the Americans.

They let us know that they had found the American lines. We wanted to leave immediately, but they stopped us. The younger one sat down and made a sweeping circular motion with his hand. When his hand reached the floor, he said something in German, which Willis thought meant we'd go when it was dark. Daylight was already nearly spent, but the younger boy continued to sit, and his older companion joined him on the floor. Neither the boys nor we knew whether to completely trust each other. They continued to sit on the floor, silently and suspiciously watching us, so we sat down and watched them!

Finally the younger boy rose from the floor and said, "OK!" They'd picked up that word easily. He indicated that we were to walk in single file and to be totally quiet. Motioning us to follow, they emerged from the barn and started in a direction that I felt was wrong. "No, American," I said. They nodded their heads in agreement and pointed in a different direction than I would have chosen. "American," they said, nodding their heads and smiling. Were they leading us straight to the Germans?

The shorter boy led the way and began to zigzag through the woods and underbrush. By now, darkness had settled, and we often had to stop and crouch down in the darkness, fearing we might be detected.

"Are we fools for trusting them?" I whispered to Willis.

"Who knows? You better start praying, Chaplain," he replied.

The moon was out again, and this time there were no clouds. Soon we reached what appeared to be a trail wide enough for a car. The boys started jogging, so we jogged along behind them. Their jog turned into a run, and we ran to keep up with them. A few minutes after the sound of flowing water joined the pounding of our boots, we arrived at the water's edge. The river was quite wide at this point and fairly shallow. If we could cross it, we'd surely be near the American line.

Cautiously, the shorter boy looked up and down the river, then rolled up his pant legs and waded across. The taller boy followed suit. Once across, they motioned for us to follow. Having watched the lads cross, I figured our boot tops were higher than the water level, so we didn't remove them. Willis went first, then my splashing boots made their way to the other bank.

The trail continued on this side of the river. Now the boys slowed to a quick jog, and we proceeded for about an hour with no one saying a word. The only sounds were our breathing, our feet pounding on the narrow road, and an occasional brush of our legs against a bush. I was praying the whole time, because I felt responsible for Willis as well as myself.

Suddenly a voice pierced the darkness like a sharp knife. "Halt! Who goes there?" The voice spoke perfect English, but we knew that the Germans were very good at tricking Americans to surrender by posting English-speaking soldiers at their outposts. We remained totally silent and unmoving. Once again the voice in the darkness spoke. "Who goes there? You are surrounded. Advance slowly and be identified."

Rather reluctantly, I responded, "I am Sergeant Charles White, an American chaplain. I'm accompanied by my driver and two German boys whom we hope are leading us to the American side. None of has any weapons. We are totally unarmed."

A long pause ensued, and then came the dreaded command: "Give the password."

The password was changed every 24 hours. If the current password was "cow," the one being challenged would respond "cow," and the sentry would then would give a counter word, such as "brown." The combination would identify both the sentry and the one challenged as Americans.

Now Willis and I had a problem. Having been gone from our unit for more than 48 hours, we hadn't a clue what the password or counter-passwords were.

"Sir," I began. We have been away from our post for over 48 hours. We became lost after we could not cross a bombed-out bridge. We don't know the password."

Suddenly four American servicemen stepped out of the bushes and surrounded us. "Show your identity," one of them demanded. Willis and I quickly showed our name tags and I showed them our maps and orders. Seemingly satisfied, they asked, "And who are these two boys?"

"As I mentioned earlier, we are trusting them to lead us to the American side," I replied. "We can't talk to them and don't know them by name. They just showed up at the barn where we were hiding." All four of us, including the boys, were marched under guard for about half a mile to a bunker where the officer in charge was stationed.

"Who are you?" he questioned. Only after I produced the orders, maps, and our ID cards did he begin to believe our story. He picked up the phone to call headquarters. "Says he is Sergeant White, a chaplain . . . yes sir." Still on the phone, he asked me, "When did you leave, and why didn't you return the same day?" he asked. Willis let me tell the story, a few sentences at a time, as the officer relayed them to headquarters.

"Yes sir," he said. Then hanging up the phone, he turned to us and announced, "They gave you up as either dead or prisoners of war. They found the jeep and trailer—what was left of them. Nothing remained in the trailer, and the jeep had been stripped of everything that was removable—headlights, tires, even the fan belts and fan! And, of course, the spark plugs and distributor were gone. You have been listed as POWs for the last 24 hours. Someone is coming from headquarters to check you out for sure."

Another officer interrogated us when the jeep from headquarters arrived. Finally, they accepted our story, and the soldiers were dismissed back to their posts. Before we boarded the jeep, we made sure the two boys received all the candy and other items they could carry back with them to their families. I hugged each boy and said "Danke! Danke!" which I knew meant "thank you" in German. It sounded so hollow. How could I ever thank them enough for leading us to safety! The boys waved good-bye and disappeared into the night. They could just as well have led us to a German camp. Surely God had impressed them to help us!

When Willis and I walked back into the hospital unit, the men gave a whoop of joy and ran to embrace us. Willis' crew gave him the same warm welcome.

"Great is Thy faithfulness, Great is Thy faithfulness," I sang out loud. Those who knew the song joined with me. The phrase "New mercies I see" took on a whole new meaning to me. What a letter I had to write to Mardell! But first, where was some solid food?

Chapter 25

HOME AT LAST

Daffodils and tulips began dotting the war-torn landscape with points of color. Tiny new buds on the trees waited to burst out with new leaves. Spring had arrived in Germany. The steady flow of wounded from the battlefields had slowed to a mere trickle, indicating that the war was nearing an end in Germany. It seemed clear that Germany could not continue to fight much longer. We waited for several weeks for orders to move, but none came.

Almost daily some new rumor leaped from patient to patient and staff member to staff member, electrifying the atmosphere. One rumor persisted day after day—and I heard it again as I was scrubbing in for a surgery. Doctor Black approached me.

"I heard that we would all be moved to the Pacific war zone to help with the end of the war with Japan," he said.

I stopped scrubbing for just a second. "Are you serious, sir?" I asked.

"Well, it's either that or something another reliable source told me, that our troops have been ordered to take Berlin and our field hospital will be assigned to accompany them. Take your pick."

We actually began to send our patients back to field hospitals, preparatory to our move to somewhere. But where? It was pleasant to have a more relaxed schedule, but the uncertainty of the future took its toll on our nerves.

In early May of 1945 we heard the rumor that Hitler was dead. A day or so later, we received the official news. To a Christian, anyone's death brings sadness, yet knowing the evils Hitler had perpetrated, and seeing their results firsthand in the sacrifice of so many innocent lives, I wholeheartedly joined in the celebration.

Still, we waited for directions concerning the future of our hospital unit. Soon after we had sent our last patient to a field hospital, we received the official word: "Germany has surrendered unconditionally."

Spontaneous celebrations erupted all around and continued for several days. Men from other field units near ours came to rejoice with us. Even civilians from nearby small towns, considered our enemies a few days before, danced for joy with the Americans. No longer "at war," little difference now existed between commissioned officers and enlisted men, and even between Americans and Germans.

Word of our future as a unit came a few days later. We would be deactivated. This meant that we would not be going to Japan—or anywhere else—as a unit. It also meant that all of us would either be going back to the States or sent to other units. Wondering what our future held, the entire unit gathered in loose formation to listen to the colonel.

"We give points for various things," he announced. "One point for each month of service, two points for each month overseas, 12 points if you are married, 12 points for each child, and five points for each battle star or other award received." A murmur rippled through the crowd.

"Silence! I have more to say," the colonel commanded. "Those with the highest number of points will be sent home first." I mentally calculated my points and came up with about 80. Others had points up to 300! I resigned myself to the fact that it would be several months before I could anticipate going home.

A few days later Dr. Black informed me that we had received orders to set up an occupation army. He must have noticed the puzzled expression on my face, because he went on to explain that when one country defeats another in war, the government of the defeated nation no longer exists. Thus, the victorious army has to establish a temporary government to maintain law and order and continue basic services.

"That, Dr. Black," said, "is what we Americans have to do for Germany."

I sensed that, since it would be some time before I received orders to return to the United States, I would become part of the occupation army. Dr. Black agreed that this would very likely be the case.

The American army quickly formed units throughout Germany. These units would remain for some time while the Germans set up their own democratic system after years under Hitler's dictatorship. And, as I had anticipated, those of us not yet eligible to go home would soon be assigned to these various units throughout Europe while we awaited our "magic number." Calculating that I would most likely be serving in Germany six to eight more months, I began to worry. Would I now encounter Sabbath problems?

In a few days I was transferred to an army general hospital near Haroldfurt, Germany. The commanding officer interviewed me and assigned me to serve as chaplain over three large patient wards. I found housing in a large, five-story abandoned office building that the army had confiscated and shared a small room with another hospital staffer. The building represented far more comfort than a tent, and it was near enough to the hospital that I could walk to work, taking my meals at the hospital staff dining hall.

Of more than 2,000 male patients in the hospital, relatively few were there because of wounds. The hospital mainly treated servicemen who had contracted a venereal disease through immoral contact with German women while in combat. No one could be released to leave Germany until every vestige of disease was cleared up.

I discovered that my assignment differed greatly from that of the combat field hospital. It seemed relatively easy to me; there were no nightly missions and no imminent danger of attack! I had just three large wards of patients with whom to become acquainted. Two other Protestant chaplains and I divided the weekend services and one midweek service. The Catholic chaplain set up his own schedule.

Keeping 2,000 men who were not seriously wounded—and prohibited to leave for any reason—busy with activities challenged the Social Services department. Tough army men soon tired of making cards for their families and braiding plastic strands to hold pendants and whistles. Muttered and shouted curses filled the air as the men suffered through their detention in frustration. They were prisoners until they were declared free of their disease by a panel of army physicians. Then and only then were they were transferred under careful escort directly to a ship for debarkation. The Army didn't want to take a chance on these men becoming re-infected!

We had no Jewish chaplains in the hospital. Because of Hitler's campaign to exterminate Jews during the war, Jewish chaplains did not get assigned to combat units in Europe for fear they might be taken captive. When the Jewish hospital personnel and patients learned that I was a Seventh-day Adventist and observed their Sabbath, some of them requested that I conduct services for them. Soon we had a Friday night service, primarily for Jewish staff or patients. However, we announced that it was open to anyone who wished to attend. Twenty-five to 30 persons began to attend regularly.

For several weeks I used only the Old Testament as the basis for our study. After a few weeks I asked those attending if they would be interested in studying the Old Testament prophecies in the Bible pointing to the Messiah. They voted unanimously in favor of this, and we continued these studies for several weeks. I felt that the seed sown there would find fruitage for Christ in His eternal kingdom.

In the early fall of 1945, several weeks after I had started my work at this general hospital, I received notice of an upcoming furlough. Trips for service personnel had been arranged to London, Switzerland, or Paris. I'd already been to London. The trip to Switzerland was scheduled to last 10 days while the trip to Paris only five. *I'm getting close to the top of the list for returning home,* I thought. *I sure don't want my number to come up while I'm gone!* Consequently, I chose the shorter trip to Paris.

In late November three other men and I began our furlough with a jeep ride through the German and French countryside. Whole towns lay in almost total ruins. Piles of stone, timbers, and steel marked the spots where buildings once stood. Wrecked vehicles from both the German and American armies lay scattered along the roads, like a child's discarded toys. Ravaged towns and cities in both countries looked like ghost towns! I wondered, *Where have all the residents gone?* The few civilians we saw waved at us with friendly smiles.

I found Paris disappointing. Historic buildings that had been damaged in the war still remained closed to the public, and the untouched ones had been stripped of their beauty and historic relics. When the French realized that Germany was about to invade, they'd shipped most of their treasures out of the country for safekeeping. Even though disappointing, the trip provided a change of scenery and provided an opportunity to see much more of France and Germany than I'd seen during the war.

When I returned to base, the Army was facing a problem. Thousands of American vehicles used during the war were now stored in motor pools all over Europe. The problem was getting them safely back to the United States. The Army's solution was for discharged servicemen scheduled to return to the United States to drive a vehicle in convoy from the motor pools to the port of debarkation in southern France.

I desperately hoped I could arrive home in time for Christmas. In addition to Mardell, I had a son I'd never seen who was now more than a year old. I received my acceptance to drive a jeep from Haroldfurt to the port in southern France. All I had to do now was wait for the official order to come through giving me the date of my departure.

Sadly, Christmas came and went, and still I had received no word. "I'll be home for Christmas, if only in my dreams . . ." The carol seemed to be written with me in mind, and my dreams were certainly of Mardell, her family, and my son that holiday season. I thought of my first Christmas with Mardell and the warmth of her family that had thawed my frozen, lonely heart. *What would they be doing right now?* I thought wistfully.

Gathering around the table and reading the story of Jesus' birth? Opening presents? I had to stop thinking about it.

Two days after Christmas, my orders arrived! Before the day ended, I and several other men were headed north in a truck to Haroldfurt, about 10 hours away, where we would pick up the vehicles we were to drive to France.

We arrived at the motor pool late that night and were assigned a place to sleep. Early the next morning a bugle call awakened us and by 9:00 a.m. we had finished breakfast and were standing in the large garage where the jeeps and other vehicles were stored. Each jeep had four men assigned to it. A small steel trailer attached to the rear of the jeep carried duffel bags and other personal items. A convoy of 50 vehicles formed quickly, and we headed southwest toward France and the ship that would take us home. The convoy halted along the highway every two hours for a mandatory 10-minute break and to change drivers. At noon we stopped, and a food truck distributed the familiar C rations to each of us. In the late afternoon we pulled into a large army base, where a hot meal awaited us, and we bunked in a large tent for the night. The familiar sound of the bugler awakened us very early the next morning, and we were on our way well before daylight.

Destroyed bridges necessitated several detours, but otherwise our trip proved uneventful. Each of us realized that every turn of the wheels brought us closer to the ship that was waiting to carry us home to our loved ones. Our anticipation ran high!

Arriving at the port of debarkation, enjoying the much warmer air of southern France, we checked in our vehicles at a huge motor pool and took our luggage to a truck that carried us to the loading dock. There, we showed our identification papers three different times before being allowed to board. Oh what joy to be walking up the gangplank onto the deck of that ship! Given my experience with sea travel, I made sure I had an ample supply of antiseasick pills with me. Though crowded, the ship had more room than we had had coming from America, and I even enjoyed most of the meals! Thankfully, the ocean liner glided across the Atlantic smoothly and uneventfully.

Before dawn one morning, word passed through the ship that we would soon be close enough to see the New York skyline. I skipped breakfast and stood on deck with hundreds of others, straining for my first glimpse of the lights of New York City. Bundled up against the cold wind, no one talked, each of us wrapped in his own thoughts.

As the eastern sun lifted into a cloudless sky, someone pointed and shouted, "There it is!" In the far distance, the city skyline slowly material-

ized. After a few exclamations of recognition, silence fell again until someone cried out, "There's our lady!" I craned my neck and squinted my eyes
to see the Statue of Liberty. Many of us had never seen her, except in pictures. Along with nearly everyone else, I shamelessly wiped the tears from
my eyes. Home! Freedom! What a moving moment!

Our great ship glided silently through the waters, guided by the port
captain in his small escort boat. The silhouettes became buildings, and we
could see men moving along the wharves. They looked like tiny play toys.
As our ship neared our assigned dock, a loudspeaker crackled, "Everyone report to your cabin. Clear the decks. Wait in your cabin to be escorted to the
gangplank in order." I hated to leave the deck! Lingering as long as possible,
my eyes drank in every building, every car, every sign of life in America.

Back in my windowless cabin I waited anxiously to be escorted off the
ship. Feeling the gentle nudge of the vessel touching the wharf, I could en-
vision the navy men throwing heavy ropes to anchor us securely to the
dock. I could scarcely contain myself. I was home! I was back in America!
I had survived the war!

Again, we had to be checked and identified. Obviously, the navy men
assigned to our ship had done this many times before, and the troops were
escorted in an orderly fashion to the top of the gangplank. We showed our
identification again and received a "Welcome Home!" salute. At the bottom of the gangplank we had to show our identification one more time.
Cold winds swept the dock, but this was home! Who minded the cold?
Long tables had been set up on the dock, and Red Cross ladies offered us
doughnuts and coffee or hot chocolate. A Salvation Army band played
military music and hymns as we marched in loose formation to the busses
that would transport us to a nearby military base.

Arriving at the base, we marched in double file, loose formation, to
our barracks. Once again we had to show our identification, and then we
were assigned to a bunk in one of the barracks. I left my duffel bag and
other personal items on my bunk, then joined a large group of other men
as we gathered in formation in front of the barracks. We marched a couple of blocks to a building marked "Finance." We passed in one door, received a small amount of money, signed for it, and then left the building
through a rear door. American money! Real money! During our entire
stay overseas, we had received "occupancy money," printed for use only
during the war and during the occupation that followed.

From the finance building we marched to a giant mess hall. The tables
offered a menu such as I had never seen before and have never seen since!

The tables were laden with various meats, a large variety of vegetables, real mashed potatoes (not the powdered ones we had received overseas), and real milk. Having drunk powdered skim milk for so long, I loved the rich and creamy taste! To top the meal off, we had our choice of three desserts, including pie and ice cream. What a feast!

Back at our barracks we were told, "Do not unpack anything you do not need. There will be no more inspections, because within 48 hours you will be on your way to the army base where you were inducted." I joined the other men in a great cheer! All of us were free to go anywhere on base. However, the commanding officer advised, "Be sure to check the bulletin board just inside each barracks every hour or so. The names of those scheduled to leave will be posted constantly."

One of the first things I did was to find a pay phone and dial home. When Mardell answered, I choked up and for a minute could not speak. Only after she repeated her greeting did I find my voice. "Mardell, this is Charles."

"Oh, Charles!" she squealed! "Where are you? How are you? When will you get home?" The questions tumbled out of her mouth so fast that I didn't have time to answer even one of them.

"Darling, slow down!" I laughed. "I'm at an army base near New York City, and we've been promised to be transferred to our base of induction within two days. However, I don't know for sure when I'll leave here or when I'll arrive in Kansas. I'll call you as soon as I receive my orders," I promised. "Until then, we'll just have to wait. But it won't be long until we're together again!"

After the too-short phone call, I headed for the huge PX not far from my barracks. Rows upon rows of the latest food items greeted me. I could select from a multitude of items and buy at a discount price. I felt like a child turned loose in a cookie shop! But having bought a little something for Mardell and my son in Paris, and not wanting to carry extra weight with me, I limited myself to a newspaper.

I received my orders the next day. My service record and other important papers were sealed in an official military brown envelope. An officer handed me a train ticket to Fort Leavenworth, Kansas, where I'd been inducted more than 39 months before. I also received meal tickets to use on the train.

Stepping onto the train, my eyes scanned the railcar. Returning servicemen filled almost every seat. Most were traveling alone to various destinations, but all of us were former European war veterans, and the trip across the States carried quite a festive air.

Sooner than I'd anticipated, the train chugged into Fort Leavenworth. I received a thorough physical examination and exchanged my old military clothing for a brand new uniform and overcoat. Along with others being discharged, my records were checked, and in a brief ceremony, battle stars and other medals were awarded.

Next, I passed through another finance department where I received the remaining money due me. This included a $300 "mustering out" bonus! The last station to visit before being released was with the military recruiter. I bit my lip to keep from laughing as he invited—no, urged—me to reenlist. He promised a nice bonus and an immediate 90-day furlough. I didn't take the bait and I don't recall any others accepting, either.

Because of the war, the telephone companies in small rural areas still had party lines, making it possible for anyone to listen in on the conversations of anyone else on their line. And everybody listened to everyone else's call, so when I phoned Mardell to tell her when I'd be arriving, we were sure that Mardell and I were not talking just to each other! She and her parents decided we wanted more privacy than would be possible if a lot of neighbors showed up at the train station to meet me. They therefore chose to drive 70 miles down the tracks to a more private homecoming.

The trip across the country took several days, and my excitement grew with every passing mile. My train finally pulled out of the last station before the one where I was to meet Mardell and her parents. The conductor couldn't help noticing my eager anticipation and asked me, "Soldier, how come you are so excited?" I told him that at the next stop I would be meeting my wife, her parents, and my son whom I had never seen. As we neared that town, he said, "Get your belongings near the door. When the train stops, just get off and I'll put your things on the platform for you."

As soon as the train began to slow down, I sat motionless, staring out the window toward where the platform would soon be. My eyes didn't want to blink, for fear of missing Mardell. With a last gasp and squeal of brakes, the train ground to a stop. *There she is!* I fairly shouted to myself. The next few moments blurred as I exploded from the train. Seat back in front of me . . . aisle . . . steps . . . wooden platform . . . Mardell's arms. We wrapped each other tightly in a long embrace.

The only reason I would release her from my arms was to hug my son. My *son!* Now a toddler, Mardell's smiling mother held him out to me, and I swung him around and around, much to his delight. We all cried and laughed together. What a homecoming! Our family circle was once again complete.

Chapter 26

UNEXPECTED PHONE CALL

My son, who had seen me only in pictures, warmed up to me quickly, soon running to me and throwing his arms around my neck, exclaiming, "Daddy, Daddy!" What words can bring a greater thrill to a proud father's heart?

I arrived home from the army too late to enroll for the second semester at Union College in Lincoln, Nebraska. It felt familiar to go with Harold to the barn, milk the cow, and help gather the eggs. While Missy, the old barn kitty, may not have remembered me, she remembered the routine for sure, and when she heard the first squirts of milk hit the pail, she appeared, purring and rubbing against my leg.

For the next several days I fell into the routine of the farm, helping where I could, but restless to know what the next steps in my civilian life would be.

"Maybe we should go to Lincoln, anyway," I told Mardell. "I could get a printing job and be there to use my GI bill starting the summer term."

"That sounds reasonable to me," she concurred. Mom and Dad agreed.

After chores one morning we gathered around the table for morning worship. The sharp ringing of the phone interrupted our devotions, and Mardell jumped up to answer it.

"Hello? . . . Yes, this is Mardell, Charles' wife . . . You want to speak with Charles? May I tell him who is calling?" Her eyes, which had been focusing on random objects around the room, came to a rest on me. "Just a moment, Elder Venden, I'll get him on the line."

"Elder Venden?" I queried as I rose from my chair. "What does the president of the Nebraska Conference want with me?" I rose from the table and walked the few steps to the phone that hung on the wall between the kitchen and the living room.

"This is Charles White."

After the usual formal greetings he said, "Charles, I'd like to invite you to come to work in the Nebraska Conference as a minister."

I could hardly believe my ears. I felt speechless. Finally, I found my voice. "But sir," I stammered, "I still have two years of college work to complete. I plan to use my GI bill starting this summer. I have absolutely no experience as a minister."

"I've checked you out, White," he said. "I've talked with some of our army chaplains who know of your service overseas as a field chaplain. I've also learned that you taught a number of classes before going overseas. You served admirably in the army. I believe you can handle the job now, and I need ministers badly! The war has created a shortage, with so many ministers being inducted into the army. Could you and your wife be in my office this coming Monday morning at 9:00?"

I swallowed hard. Still reeling, I managed to blurt out the words, "Yes sir, we will be there." I could hear several clicks as one after another of our neighbors hung up. Now they all knew of my invitation to be a minister!

We borrowed Harold's car and drove the 250 miles to Lincoln. Monday morning found us in the outer office of Elder Dan Venden, president of the Nebraska Conference of Seventh-day Adventists. His office was simply but tastefully furnished. His secretary knocked on his door, and we entered his office. He wore a suit and tie, and I was glad I'd chosen to dress similarly. He showed the two of us to a couple of chairs. After a brief chat in which he inquired about my experience in the army, he turned to the business at hand. "The place I most need help is the Beatrice, Nebraska, district," he said. "It's about 35 miles from Lincoln and has four churches and one company [a particularly small congregation]. The district pastor, Elder Grooves, is quite ill and desperately needs help."

"What exactly would you expect of me?" I asked.

"In all truth, Charles, because Pastor Grooves is so ill, you would probably be responsible for almost everything—preaching alternate Sabbaths at two churches one week, and three the next. You'd hold prayer meetings, visit the members, conduct board meetings, and generally be the shepherd for the members in this area."

"But sir, I have no experience in such matters," I protested.

"Well, you held services on base, didn't you? And I heard that you visited troops within a radius of the camp, ministering to their spiritual needs. It's not a lot different here," he reassured me.

After about half an hour's discussion, we found ourselves assigned to the Beatrice, Nebraska district! We drove the 35 miles to Beatrice to meet Pastor Grooves, and I could tell that he was indeed quite ill.

The district covered the entire southeastern part of Nebraska. Before going back home, we rented an apartment. Using my mustering-out bonus from the army, we bought some essential furniture to set up housekeeping. We also bought some civilian clothes for me.

"We'll obviously need a car," I told Mardell, "but this presents a great challenge."

"Why?" she asked.

"Well, no new cars were manufactured during the entire war, and there are very few used cars available."

Praying together, we searched diligently and finally located a 1936 Graham Page in good condition. We made the down payment, again from my mustering-out money, and agreed to make monthly payments until it was ours. We traveled back to the family farm to return Harold's car with Mardell behind the wheel of her dad's car, and me driving the Graham Page.

Before we left Mardell's parents, we reveled in their company. Although we would be only 250 miles away, it felt like a final separation. Our son had never been away from his grandparents for even a night, and now, all of a sudden, we were taking him from them. On the day of our departure, we all knelt in the dining room, and Harold offered a powerful dedicatory prayer, commissioning both of us to the Lord's service. Kisses, hugs, and well-wishing perfumed the air as we finally pulled ourselves away and started down the road to Beatrice.

We quickly settled into the routine of speaking at two churches one Sabbath, then at two others and the company the following Sabbath. We had to leave home early enough to arrive at the first church by 9:00 a.m. Right after my sermon, we jumped in the car and traveled another 60 miles to preach at the second church at 11:30, then on to the third group for a 2:30 service. We obviously had to decline invitations to have lunch with our members, instead eating our lunch in the car as we drove to the third place.

Pastor Grooves continued to struggle with serious illness. He spent nearly all of his time in bed, and I gained most of my "intern training" at his bedside. During the week Mardell and I visited the homes of our members, our schedule much more relaxed than on Sabbaths. Many of our members enjoyed playing with our son, too.

One day, about a year into our service in the Beatrice district, I prepared to visit some members who lived out in the country. Mardell opted to stay home and get caught up with some things around the house.

As I started the engine, I thought I heard the car make a noise that I hadn't heard before. Not being a mechanic, I didn't even know what to check for, and since it was running, I eased out of the driveway and onto the road leading out of town. After about 30 minutes, I turned onto a gravel road, enjoying the beautiful spring scenes on all sides. As I started up a fairly steep incline, the car began to complain—loudly. Gurrrr . . . gurrr! Clank . . . clank!

What in the world . . .? I wondered. Just as I crested the hill, my Graham Page let out one last angry protest, and before I could even stop the car, the engine died.

I coasted to a stop on the side of the road. I got out and lifted the hood, more as a sign for help than because I could identify the problem. Had it been a printing press malfunctioning, I could easily have spotted and diagnosed the problem, but car engines were foreign to me! Fifteen minutes passed with no other motorists in sight. Finally, an old car carrying an even older farmer approached, so I flagged him down and hitched a ride into the nearest town. There I arranged for the car to be towed into the garage. The mechanic soon discovered the problem—a broken piston rod had driven a hole into the engine block!

Checking the local bus schedule, I saw that one would be leaving for Beatrice late that afternoon. I called Mardell and told her the problem and that I'd be on the late afternoon bus.

It seems incredible, but the very next day, God led me to a low-mileage, 1939 Chevrolet! Miracles still poured from God's heavenly storehouse! The car looked great, had good tires, and ran like new. That car served us for more than two years, when we were able to buy our first new car.

Throughout the rest of the spring and the hot Nebraska summer, we kept busy visiting members, preaching, and ministering to our flock. I loved my work but began to feel restless. I had a GI bill for college and felt it would improve my ministry if I had more education. Mardell and I frequently dreamed about returning to Union College, but the demands of the district kept us too busy to think much about it.

As September 1946 approached, Mardell said to me one day, "Charles, you need to go back to college and finish up your degree. You have the GI bill. It'd pay your tuition and most of your other college expenses."

"Not only that," I continued, "it would also provide a small amount for living expenses. But you know how deeply involved I am in this work. I thoroughly enjoy everything required of me. Besides, our district pastor is failing. He's due to retire the end of this year. I feel that the Lord is blessing us and leading us."

140

"Well, why don't we talk with Elder Venden and seek his advice?" she asked. We arranged for a meeting with Elder Venden.

On the appointed day we arrived at the conference office a bit early and climbed the stairs to the president's office on the second floor. We killed some time looking at pictures in the hallway, then entered his secretary's office a few minutes before the hour.

"We have an appointment with Elder Venden in a few minutes," I told the secretary. "We can just wait here in your office until he is ready to see us."

"Is that you, White?" Elder Venden called out. He'd apparently heard us talking with his secretary. "Come on in!"

After we were comfortably seated, I cleared my throat and began my speech: "Elder Venden, we thoroughly enjoy the pastoral ministry and the people in our district. However, I do have a GI bill for schooling, and I am convinced that a sharpened tool is more effective than a dull one. I would like to request a leave of absence so I can enroll full-time at Union College, beginning this fall semester."

A cloud of disappointment obscured the light in his eyes. "Please stay on in the ministry," he urged. "If you stay, I will see to it that you are ordained with or without a college degree, and I'll be happy to apply your experience as army chaplain to your internship."

We chatted a bit longer, and then I said, "Give us some time to pray about your offer. It does sound inviting, but we'd like to consult with our Chief before we make a decision."

"Certainly," Venden agreed. "Such weighty decisions need prayer and heavenly guidance. Just know that we are very pleased with your work, and I again ask you to stay on with us."

It *did* sounded inviting. Mardell and I talked about it all the way home, weighing the pros and cons. On one hand, if I returned to school, I would miss out on Elder Venden's generous offer, which would most likely never be duplicated if he should move to another jurisdiction. On the other hand, with all the benefits of the GI bill, I would never have a better opportunity to return to Union College than now.

After several days of serious prayer and deliberation, I phoned the president.

"Elder Venden," I said, "I really am strongly impressed that I should continue my education. Therefore, I will submit my resignation effective two weeks before the fall semester begins."

He reluctantly agreed.

We located a basement apartment in Lincoln and moved in. When I registered, I learned that it would take me two full years plus one summer to complete all the requirements for my degree. I signed up for a full load of classes and also took a part-time job working at the college press. After five years of being out of school I was a college student again.

Daily classes, homework, work at the press, and family responsibilities kept me running. However, in the midst of my hectic schedule, I felt a soft but determined nudging in my mind, and it would not leave me alone. In honest moments, I had to admit that I missed the pastoral ministry I had pursued for most of the previous year. *My members don't have a pastor! Who's caring for their needs? Who's conducting their services?*

"Mardell," I said one day about two weeks into the school year, "I can't tell you how unhappy I am! It's not the classes, the homework, or my hectic schedule so much. I just miss preaching every week and all the other parts of the ministry. Here at Union College I'm just another student, not needed by anyone. We go to the church services, but we have no active part. My heart is still back in the district with the people I've grown to love."

"I think I understand," Mardell agreed. "It's just not the same, is it?"

On Monday of the third week, I felt a deep impression to go over to the conference office and talk with Elder Venden. During a mid-morning break in classes, I walked across the street to his office. Entering his secretary's office, I asked if the president was able to see me, and he heard me talking. His voice boomed out: "What took you so long, White? Come in here!"

There was no small talk this time. I came right to the point. "Sir," I said, "I miss the preaching. I miss visiting with members. I miss the daily challenges, and I miss feeling needed. Is there anything I can do while attending school?"

"White, you are an answer to prayer!" he exclaimed. "We're dividing the large district into two separate ones, and you could take the district nearest to Union College. You would be pastor of the Beatrice and the Nebraska City churches."

I resigned from the press, since the income from part-time ministry would more than make up for the income from that job. Our goodbyes to the Beatrice members became a joyful "Hello again!" For the next two years and the summer sessions between semesters I served these two churches each weekend and as often as possible during the week.

During my last year in college the same religion department that had warned me that I would never make a minister assigned three ministerial students to assist me and to train in holding a public evangelistic crusade— a miracle for a "no-good" boy who would "never amount to anything!"

God continued working miracles throughout my years in the ministry. He moved us from familiar Nebraska all over the eastern and southern United States and blessed us in every endeavor.

Is it not a miracle that a "no-good" boy who was hesitant in speech would become a daily and weekly radio speaker? Is it not a miracle that the boy with the bitter heart would grow up to work alongside God in removing bitterness from human hearts? Is it not a miracle that the boy who was labeled as "stupid" grew up to lead nine congregations in building new churches and schools? This "failure" had been transformed by a miracle of God's grace.

EPILOGUE

Ever since my encounter with God in the tree grove way back in my teens, I had known in my heart that God wanted me to serve Him as a minister. Everyone I knew was convinced that it would never work, including me. But ultimately, it wasn't their decision or my decision. Against all odds, God polished and groomed an imperfect instrument for His service, working miracle after miracle in the process.

From training army recruits in the basics of first aid to becoming an army chaplain to becoming a full time minister, God grew me into becoming His worker. As I review my life, I remain convinced that if God wants you to do something for Him, and if you are willing, that's where you're going to be. You can do anything—become anything—because you serve the God of miracles.

Since my retirement in 1981, I haven't slowed down much. I have been privileged to: serve as interim pastor in four churches; travel from Florida to Canada and from the Missouri River to the Atlantic ocean holding five- to six-week evangelistic campaigns; speak at spiritual retreats; spend 15 months in Seoul, South Korea, keeping the Seventh-day Adventist Servicemen's Center (a "home away from home" for our servicemen) open and serve as a civilian chaplain; lead a building program for a new church; and serve as chaplain of a large health-care facility.

I have nothing to boast about in any of this. I thank God every day for the measure of health that allowed me to be active for Him until 2004. I thank Him that miracles still continue to shower my daily life. I say with the apostle Paul, "I can do all things through Christ which strengtheneth me" (Philippians 4:13).

I have had to slow down—way down! After suffering from a stroke I could no longer navigate at home, so I now pass my days in a long-term care center. My faithful wife comes every day to visit me, and we both eagerly await the greatest miracle of our lives when "This mortal shall put on immortality" and I'll see Jesus face to face.